Years of Estrangement

YEARS *of* ESTRANGEMENT

ERICH LEYENS · LOTTE ANDOR

Translated by Brigitte Goldstein

Prefaces by Wolfgang Benz

NORTHWESTERN UNIVERSITY PRESS

Evanston, Illinois

Northwestern University Press
Evanston, Illinois 60208-4210

Originally published in German under the title *Die fremden Jahre: Erinnerungen an Deutschland.* Copyright © 1991 by Fischer Taschenbuch Verlag, GmbH, Frankfurt am Main. English translation copyright © 1996 by Brigitte Goldstein. Published 1996 by Northwestern University Press. All rights reserved.

Printed in the United States of America

ISBN 0-8101-1181-0 (CLOTH)
ISBN 0-8101-1166-7 (PAPER)

Library of Congress Cataloging-in-Publication Data

Fremden Jahre. English
  Years of Estrangement / Erich Leyens and Lotte Andor.
    p. cm. — (Jewish lives)
    Contents: Under the Nazi regime / Erich Leyens — Memoirs of an unknown actress / Lotte Andor.
    ISBN 0-8101-1181-0 (cloth : alk. paper). — ISBN 0-8101-1166-7 (pbk. : alk. paper)
    1. Leyens, Erich, 1898– . 2. Andor, Lotte, 1903–1991. 3. Jews—Germany —Biography. 4. Jews—Germany—History— 1933–1945. 5. Refugees, Jewish—United States—Biography. 6. Germany—Biography. 7. United States—Biography. I. Leyens, Erich, 1898– . Unter dem NS-Regime. English. II. Andor, Lotte, 1903–1991. Memoiren einer unbekannten Schauspielerin. English. III. Title. IV. Series.
  DS135.G5A133 1996
  943'.004924—dc20   96-33080
                                                        CIP

Contents

UNDER THE NAZI REGIME

Experiences and Observations, 1933–38

Erich Leyens

❖

Preface to *Under the Nazi Regime*

WOLFGANG BENZ

Preserved in the archives of the Leo Baeck Institute in New York is a leaflet, dated April 1, 1933, which a German Jew had handed out that day to passersby in the street in front of his department store in the town of Wesel. Distributing the leaflet was an act in defiance of the boycott staged by the Nazis against Jewish businesses, and it was an act greeted with approval by the general population of the town and by the press. The Nazi regime had come to power in Germany only a few months earlier, and its uniformed storm troopers had taken up threatening positions in front of Jewish-owned stores all over the country to enforce the boycott. In the spring of 1933, however, it was still possible to openly express solidarity with Jewish fellow citizens. Unconditional, enthusiastic surrender to the Nazi regime was still being kept within bounds.

The majority of German non-Jews, however, did not express solidarity with the Jews. It would be unrealistic to expect such an attitude given a situation in which a man who was the leader of a party that for years had noisily proclaimed anti-Semitism the core of its party program—and had done so with unconcealed brazenness in the coarsest manner—could become chancellor. But some civil decency still existed early on, and there were people who did not acquiesce sheepishly, people who would openly express sympathy for the persecuted Jews rather than merely defend them surreptitiously behind locked doors. Such cases still existed up to the time of the November 1938 pogrom. Later, when Jews were branded by being forced to wear a yellow star (starting in September 1941), when they were deported to death camps in the East, the only thing left to do for those who were not directly touched, even if they did not approve of the hateful actions taken against the Jews, apparently was

3

to look the other way, not acknowledging what was happening and denying outright the terrible reality.

In the spring of 1933, when the first sweeping public action against the Jews was being launched, the situation was still somewhat in flux. Appeals to a sense of justice and law, to social morality, or to plain civil decency could still find an echo. It was such an appeal that the Jewish businessman Erich Leyens made on April 1, 1933, and it met with great success. But only a short while later, he, too, had to resign himself to the inevitable and choose exile. After an initial stay in Italy, he attempted to make his way, without resources or recourse, in countries where he first had to learn the language, until, after seven years of wandering, he found a safe haven in the United States. Even there he was forced for years to move from job to job, all for meager wages. In the end, he was able to make it. Through hard work he established a secure existence that permitted him to alternate residences between New York and a senior citizens' home in Constance, Germany. "How many didn't make it and were cut down along the way," he wrote; then, looking back, he added: "Do you know that in San Francisco alone, six German-Jewish lawyers counted themselves happy that they had landed jobs as elevator operators? Giannini, the founder of the then-largest bank in America, was on a cordial first-name basis with his elevator operator, whom he had known as a banker in Berlin."

Erich Leyens's report, which is neither memoir nor autobiography and focuses primarily on the five years of his direct personal encounter with the Nazi regime, resulted from lifelong reflections on the destruction of culture and humanity, morality and justice, and the morale of the general population in Hitler's Germany. Questions of how a band of criminals should have been able to seize the reins of government, the ideology that was advanced for this purpose, and the social and economic conditions that contributed to it were not uppermost in the mind of this former German patriot and decorated World War I veteran. Rather, at the center of his concern was the question of how such a regime was able to rally a following and the enthusiastic endorsement of educated, otherwise morally upright citizens. How, he asked, could friends and neighbors, fellow citizens and public officials, the high school teacher or the local baker, undergo such a complete transformation? How could the masses of Germans become disposed to submit unconditionally to the Hitler cult? How could they not only become blind and impervious to the suffering of the Jewish minority, but adopt the arrogance and ruthlessness of a master race toward the neighboring nations?

Nothing reflects this transformation of civilized citizens into monstrous beings more clearly than the conference that took place on January 20, 1942, in a mansion at Wannsee in Berlin. Summoned by SS Colonel Reinhard Heydrich, the representatives of the key ministries and bureaucratic agencies of the Reich came together: high-ranking civil servants, administrators, military leaders—all of them part of the educated elite of Germany, which had reached the zenith of its power. Heydrich made clear to the gathering what had long been decided: The "final solution of the Jewish question" was at hand. The points of discussion at the Wannsee mansion concerned transportation capacities and logistical problems, that is, the technical aspects of mass murder. Those present listened calmly to the reading off of the numbers of the Jews who were to be "caught" in every part of Europe, including neutral countries. The hierarchy of population size that was established and discussed at Wannsee was monstrous: almost three million in the Ukraine, more than two million in the "General Gouvernement" of Poland, down to 330,000 Jews living in Great Britain. All in all, eleven million Jews on the entire European continent were to be exterminated. Top authorities of the Reich, by no means all fanatical Nazis, and their executive offices took note of the plan and did not cry out, but carried out what they considered their duty, thus assisting from their desks in the murder of six million Jews.

How it was possible that human beings such as those present in the conference room—the Wannsee Conference was neither the first nor the last gathering at which the logistics of mass murder were discussed—could spend a few hours planning, deciding, and organizing the deportation and murder of other human beings—who simply had the "misfortune" of being born Jews—will always remain a gruesome puzzle. For these bureaucrats and decision makers, planners and organizers, were not at all destructive characters or by nature debilitated criminal types. They were educated, refined citizens who went home and played Beethoven and read Goethe, people whose moral principles were firmly established—but alas, only within their own circle. With regard to others, they turned into barbarians.

This enigma of civil morality is what Erich Leyens tackles in his report. He continually probes these questions: Was his act of public protest on April 1, 1933, meaningless or understandable? Should he have been arrested or killed for disturbing the peace of the new order? How was he to judge the decision of his friend Hermann van den Bruck, who visited the Jew Erich Leyens in 1933 to inform him of his decision to join the Nazi Party, even to ask for the friend's understanding? And what of the attitude taken by Richard Schüren, another friend, who visited Leyens regularly to show his solidarity? Was Richard's course foolish, admirable, dangerous, or what? Was the Church's silence in the face of the discrimination against the Jews, their persecution, and ultimate extermination understandable? Was this something that should be approved or disapproved? Was it known how many "mixed marriages" there were between Jews and non-Jews in Germany? What could an ordinary mortal know in Germany about the transports that took the Jews to an unknown destination? Who had seen such deportations take place and who had heard about them? Who knew about the extermination camps at Auschwitz, Treblinka, Sobibor, and Maidanek, to name only a few?

The cardinal question, which Erich Leyens poses at the end of his report—when he left the city of his fathers where nobody even gave a sign of recognition, where nobody dared to greet him—comes down to this: Did those in power succeed in rendering good human beings into unfeeling, hard-hearted humans, heedless of the suffering of their fellows? Was it possible to see in the behavior of his former fellow citizens proof for the victory of the Nazi ideology? Was this the German of the future?

Erich Leyens would be deeply grateful were the reader to take an open, unrestrained position in exploring his questions. He promises to answer to the best of his ability any further questions that may be brought up for discussion. Readers should address letters to:

ERICH LEYENS
C/O THOMPSON
5344 STANFORD DRIVE
NASHVILLE, TN 37215

UNDER THE NAZI REGIME

After more than half a century,
And from a distance of thousands of miles,
The world that appears in these pages
Seems foreign to me.

No longer recognizable is the boy
Who fought with faith and zeal
In World War I
As a German.

Unfamiliar, too, is the man
Who lived in agony and despair
Under the Nazi regime
As a Jew.

And yet:
I dedicate
These painful memories
To the German Jew
Who I was.

NEW YORK, MAY 1990

The following account seeks to record certain events that took place during the first five years of the Nazi regime and their effect on Jewish Germans. It is also an attempt to call to mind the still bewildering, abject abyss of this period, which changed Germany forever. Although this is not intended to be an autobiographical account, a merely impersonal report could be interpreted as fiction, whereas the personal "I" speaks as witness to an epoch. Beyond this, I dare hope to encourage the unencumbered reader of a new generation to contemplate that which became possible—and why—and maybe even arouse his or her empathy . . .

The German poet Goethe once said, "I love the one who desires the impossible."

A brief discussion of the situation of the Jews in Germany before the fateful year 1933 may be helpful. History books record a steadily growing anti-Semitism in the years after World War I. It is true that such sentiments were being stirred up by certain groups hostile to the young democracy. But it was only when Hitler was nominated chancellor that these bacilli could be made virulent. Before this time, the Jews, whose ancestors had resided in Germany for countless generations, saw themselves as citizens, with equal rights, of the country of their birth. They believed that their fellow citizens of the Catholic and Protestant faiths regarded them this way as well.

A few personal episodes from my life will illustrate better than generalized observations how much the Jewish citizens of my native city of Wesel felt they were at home in Germany.

On April 13, 1930, my father, Hermann Leyens, died. On the day of his funeral, all business activity in the streets of the town practically came to a standstill. The newspapers carried extensive obituaries recognizing the great contributions he had made to the life of the town. Detailed descriptions made clear the reasons why he had been such a beloved and admired citizen.

On April 1, 1933, I stood in the street, next to a group of SA men in uniform, and distributed leaflets to the passersby. The SA were the storm troopers, organized along military lines, of the Nazi Party. A short while before, on January 30, 1933, the party had obtained certain key ministries in a newly formed government; as a result, the SA were able to rule the streets—even the regular police force had to follow their orders.

On the evening of March 31, I had been alerted to the fact that the SA were being mobilized for a boycott of Jewish businesses in the entire Reich. The next day, SA men blocked buildings decried as "Jewish." Pickets carrying hate banners were planted in front of "Jewish" stores as well as the offices of Jewish doctors and lawyers. In actuality, the Nazi demonstrators did not restrict their actions to turning away prospective customers from Jewish-owned stores; even the sick were barred from entering "Jewish" clinics for medical treatment.

It was an action felt by countless numbers of Jews as a personal humiliation to such a degree that they considered their lives robbed of all meaning. On this day began the ever-rising incidence of suicide . . .

My first reaction was to quickly design a leaflet in which I outlined the patriotic services of generations of my family to their country. That very night I found a printer, J. Ingendaay, who had the courage to print the copies and have them ready by morning. I had no doubt that I might be killed in the course of distributing these leaflets. But I was convinced that only an open stand, before their very eyes, would cure my fellow citizens of their misguided faith in the new race ideology. In the profound agitation in which I spent the night, my deep conviction became strongly associated with a desire to die.

At ten o'clock in the morning, two SA men were posted at the front entrance to our department store. And there I was with my leaflets, right beside them. I had put on my old field uniform with my war medals, and next to them was sewn the yellow "Jews' patch," as the Nazi press had been demanding. ("Wear it with pride, the yellow patch," read the headline of a Jewish newspaper. This was years before the actual decree that forced all Jews to wear a yellow star.)

What happened then proved how wrong my assumptions about my fellow citizens had been. They still showed their true thinking openly. At first, a few people stopped and observed the strange spectacle in disbelief. Then they read my leaflet with obvious shock. Soon several youngsters came running up to me and asked for a few stacks of the leaflets to hand out in other parts of town. More and more people gathered around until there were so many that the street traffic was disrupted. Voices were raised, loud and clear, in support of the statement in the leaflet. Men gave vent to their indignation. Women, crying, came up and hugged me. One neighbor, a member of the old local family Honnerbach, called the bystanders into his house to show them a book of the Wesel Regiment 43. He opened it to the page with my picture and a caption about me. The famous German march composer Blankenburg pushed his way through the line of SA men, bought a small item, and insisted that it be wrapped in the largest box with the name of the firm clearly visible. He demonstratively walked about town with the package and finally took it to the Nazi table of regulars at the Hotel Dornbusch restaurant.

The SA men remained in front of the door but made no move. Only once was a bundle of leaflets knocked out of my hand. I returned immediately with a new pack, and this time they left me alone. The tense standoff was finally resolved when the SA men received orders to withdraw.

The next day, all three local newspapers still had the courage (probably for the last time) to run stories that condoned my action against the political power, even though it had already become dominant in every area. Here is what the largest of the local newspapers wrote:

Self-Help by a Jewish Front Veteran

When people in uniform attempted to block the entrance to the commercial building of the firm Leyens & Levenbach in Wesel, one of the owners, Erich Leyens, a frontline volunteer and recipient of the Iron Cross, First Class, put on his field uniform and medals, placed himself next to the SA men, and distributed the following leaflet:

"Our Reich Chancellor Hitler, the Reich Ministers Frick and Göring have repeatedly made the following declaration: *Anyone who insults a combat veteran in the Third Reich will be punished with imprisonment!*

"All three Leyens brothers served as volunteers on the front. They were wounded and were decorated for courageous action. Their father [Hermann] Leyens had been a volunteer in the fight against the Spartacists [a radical group of militant precursors of the Communist Party in 1919]. His grandfather was wounded at Katzbach during the Wars of Liberation [1812–14]. With such a record of past national service, do we now have to be subjected to public humiliation? Is this how the fatherland today expresses its gratitude, by placing huge pickets in front of our door with the demand not to buy from our house? We regard this action, which goes hand in hand with the dissemination of slanderous accusations all over town, as an attack on our national and civic honor as well as a desecration of the memory of 12,000 German front soldiers of the Jewish faith who gave their lives in action. Furthermore, we regard this provocation as an affront against every decent citizen. We have no doubt that, even today, there are citizens in Wesel who have the courage of their convictions, which Bismarck once called for, and exemplify German integrity which, especially now, stands steadfastly by our side."

Leyens's determined and courageous action received widespread sympathy and approval from the citizenry. The business was not closed down, and open demands for a boycott also ceased shortly thereafter.

In December 1989, an eyewitness account about those days came to my attention. Rudolf Holthaus, a former employee of my company, wrote a letter to his mother in Westphalia on April 1, 1933. This letter was found among the woman's personal effects after her death. I must deny myself the pleasure of reproducing verbatim this amazing document because it contains the expression of sentiments that I personally find so moving, they belong only in private correspondence. However, even a summary of the objective observations, to which I must limit myself, reaches far beyond a mere account of what happened to my company or in Wesel. May these observations compel us to reflect on the beginnings of a perilous time.

"The employees could barely trust their eyes," the letter states, "when they saw from the windows of the upper floor a large crowd of people gathered in front of the building. In their midst was Herr L. [Mr. Leyens], in his field-gray combat uniform, next to the SA men who blocked the entrance to the store. He was handing out leaflets to the passersby. Inside, a hundred employees, with fearful, dejected faces, were standing around with nothing to do. All were concerned about their livelihood. When Herr L. came in from the street for more leaflets, he called together his personnel for a brief conference and said: 'Nobody need worry about the future.' He assured us the store would not be closed, and 'as long as we have a dry piece of bread, nobody will be dismissed.' And turning toward me, he said it was better to suffer injustice than to do it.

"Among the whippersnappers in uniform, who kept our customers at bay, we saw a young man whom Herr L. had given, not so long before, a pair of trousers, underwear, and so forth. Anyone who ever fell on hard times would turn right away to the Leyens family, and help was always forthcoming.

"In the afternoon, four wandering musicians came into the store. They played the mandolin, for a few pennies. 'Our Erich' walks over, takes a mandolin, and plays 'O Germany, High in Honor.' There wasn't a single one among us who wasn't touched and close to tears."

I, too, feel moved. After fifty-seven years, I am touched by the spirit of this letter. But I am also surprised to find details I had long forgotten mentioned in this account. How admirable it appears to me today that in this new political climate, an adolescent son proves his decency to his mother. Today, thanks to this private testimony, I am able to view the events of this perilous day through eyes other than my own. But I regret my own lack of presence of mind: How wonderful it would have been had I appeared in the street with the entire staff (whose esprit de corps was quite obvious) and exhorted the crowd to join in singing "O Germany, High in Honor." The next stanza of this old song speaks of the "holy land of faithfulness." It is likely that even the young men in brown uniforms would have joined in with enthusiasm, though unaware of its sad significance.

It would be a mistake to draw broader conclusions for all of Germany from the failure of the boycott in one small town. On the contrary, these events were proof positive that the Nazi Party already had the ability to launch a well-organized surprise action without encountering any resistance from the populace. It should also be noted that the local police lacked the courage to assure the safety of the Jewish citizens. Everywhere the police obeyed those whom they had regarded, just a short while before, as disturbers of the peace, and who now were left free to carry out the orders of the new powers-that-be.

A decisive change took place among large numbers of people: enthusiasm for an infallible leader was a new experience for Germany. Only Fascist Italy and Communist Russia could serve as models.

"Il Duce ha sempre ragione!" ("The leader is always right!") was the slogan of Mussolini's Italy. Stalin, Lenin's successor, was able to maintain power in his huge country through a reign of terror, and he remained until his death the revered dictator.

The German people, traditionally subservient to authority and politically naive, were exposed for the first time to the drumbeat of a masterful, effective propaganda machine. How could any other viewpoint besides the official one be heard if every newspaper and every radio program had to follow the guidelines of the newly created ministry for "the people's enlightenment and propaganda"? Josef Goebbels, who headed the department, had far-reaching powers over all media. Although television had not yet been invented, even theaters and museums came under his jurisdiction.

During the decisive early years, a rising tide of legislation and decrees, among them countless secret decrees, overturned the existing social order. *Gleichschaltung* (leveling) was a harmless euphemism for what was in reality legal dispossession. A characteristic example (outside the private sector) were the German trade unions, whose independent, financially strong organizations had earned them worldwide admiration. Now they were being "leveled," that is, subordinated to the Nazi Party. The same happened just as quickly, without meeting resistance, to every single economic and academic organization.

The masses of the people were seduced through the elaborate, glittering pageantry of demonstrations, performances, and parades. In the atmosphere thus created, gullible human beings were convinced that they were following new national values. Ideas like Thoreau's duty to refuse obedience in the face of blatant, immoral laws or Gandhi's nonviolent resistance, which was to defeat the British world empire, could not be voiced. Pacifists were decried as traitors to the fatherland. This was the time when General Erich

Ludendorff, the adulated hero of the world war, is reported to have said that he hated Christianity because it was Jewish and international and because of its cowardly advocacy of peace on earth.

A new archenemy was created by brilliant party demagogues. This time it was not France, which, according to Hitler, would always remain hostile, no matter which French party happened to be in power. The old canard of an "international Jewish conspiracy" was given more elaborate form and became the central message of Nazism to the nation: In the East, there was "Jewish" Bolshevism; in the West, the "Jewish" democracies, a degenerate type of government created and dominated by Jews. To combat this trend, providence dispatched a Führer to the German people, a leader as he appears only once in a thousand years. In fact, his most faithful followers saw in him the incarnation of the German soul and in the Nazi movement a form of national religion through which Germany would be redeemed and freed of all evil adversaries. I have seen with my own eyes, in religious shrines that frequently line the rural roads, a picture of Hitler replacing traditional images of the Madonna.

Again, one should not draw general conclusions from all of this. The majority of Christians disapproved of blasphemous excesses of this kind, even if they did not speak out publicly. But it is amazing and impressive how quickly the virus spread. For many, "Heil Hitler" became the accepted "German" greeting, equivalent, and in logical succession, to "Grüß Gott" ("God be greeted").

The lives of the Jews became ever more restricted by a series of exclusionary laws. First, all Jews were denied equality under the law. Then they were deprived, step by step, of their jobs. Professionals of every type were affected: physicians, lawyers, judges, civil servants, office and factory workers, everywhere, in every town and village. Soon, President Paul von Hindenburg's supposed demand for the exemption of frontline soldiers from the exclusionary policies was simply disregarded. The German Rechtsstaat (constitutional state) came to an end.

A theory, proclaimed as science, was taught at universities and in public schools, and was hammered incessantly into the national consciousness by various media: The "enemy of the people" had to be destroyed, that is, the non-Aryan element within the national body of Germany. The notion of collective guilt came into being ("the

Jews are our misfortune"). The reigning majesty of law among civilized nations, which purports that only individual guilt can be punished, was no longer in force for the Jews.

The duty I feel to recapture in writing what I have experienced and observed in the fateful first years of the Nazi regime is a painful task. It seems to me almost impossible to explain to someone born afterward the incomprehensible, today unimaginable, series of events that took place. But I shall try to write as thoroughly and objectively as I can about the amazing contradictions in that past, now distant but still vivid in my memory. I hesitated at first, and while I was still reluctant, a friend told me about a Navajo song that goes: "Tell everybody what you have seen. That which you leave unspoken will return to the circling winds." The other incident that finally prompted me to write occurred during a visit to Germany. A friend asked me to think about a saying from the Russia of Tolstoy: "Don't dig up the past; if you wallow too much in it, you'll lose one eye. But if you forget, you'll lose both and you'll have to face the future blind."

I shall relate three episodes that will illustrate the social and political climate in Germany at the time when the Nazi regime was first established.

Hermann van den Bruck had become my friend during World War I. His brother Helmut had died next to me at Verdun. We were both eighteen years old. Hermann was obviously embarrassed when he visited me one night in 1933. He began to talk about the past. Helmut had told him about the gas attack before La Bassée in September 1915. He related how we both—gas masks were not yet available then—saved our lives by urinating on scraps of cloth torn from our underwear and pressing them against our faces.

Hermann spoke about the day we first met, which was at Helmut's funeral. He himself had arrived, so he said, as a member of the regiment's staff, "all spit and polish," while I had been staggering through a muddy ravine, ducking enemy fire, and taking cover every few feet. One of my boots had gotten stuck in the mire. He said I had been an upsetting sight for the squeaky-clean comrades from positions behind the lines. The status-conscious sergeant in charge had derided me in front of everybody for my filthy appearance. Hermann said I had passed out, and he had to console me instead of I him. After an embarrassed silence, Hermann told me, his visit had a more painful purpose than reminiscing about the old days. It had to do with the complete change of the spirit of the times. He had come to tell me personally that he was about to become a member of the Nazi Party. For him, he explained, there simply was no way around it. If he did not join the party, his business would also be boycotted and he would be ruined. His duty to his family did not permit him to run such a risk. He also could no longer see me; he could not even greet me in the street.

To this day I can feel the paralyzing numbness that gripped me. For a long while I was unable to speak. Then I was foolish enough to remind him of a conversation we once had about "expediency as a principle of the devil." This was a phrase coined by Walther Rathenau, a Jew, who had been murdered by forerunners of the Nazis.[*] But then I realized that Hermann was struggling to hold back the tears and that he now was more in need of being consoled than I.

Later, during a sleepless night, I tried to figure out why this encounter had left me so frightened and weighed so heavily on me. After all, I should not take it too hard to have lost this friend. If a friend does not prove his mettle in hard times, was he truly a friend? I came to the bitter conclusion that Hermann was a decent human being, a deeply religious Christian, a member of an old, highly respected Wesel family—pious, upright folk for generations. If a

---

[*]The name Rathenau may mean little nowadays, but one would do well to remember it. Walther Rathenau took over the responsibilities of the office of foreign minister of the Weimar Republic, against the advice of friends, at a most difficult time in German history—and in 1922 he was murdered. There was a song at the time, popular among the forerunners of the Nazis: "Let's kill that Walther Rathenau, that goddamn, filthy Jew sow."

Rathenau was an engineer and a successful industrialist. He was also the author of many books of lasting value on national economy and philosophy. He was an ardent patriot, the only one who in 1918, after the armistice, called for a "levée en masse" (a spontaneous uprising of the people). Later, when he became foreign minister, he restored respect and honor to Germany with his "Pace-Pace" speech at the Geneva conference and placed before the Western powers the first comprehensive economic treaty of the postwar period. Rathenau had already, in 1913, proposed an economic union of the Western countries as a precondition for peace. He envisioned a United States of Europe as a logical, inevitable development. Today the question poses itself whether both world wars could have been avoided had he been taken seriously.

man as kind and honorable as Hermann saw himself forced to participate in this fanatical political movement, what did it mean for the future?

Richard Schüren came to my house at least twice a week during these unsettled times following the April 1933 boycott. We had never had any private dealings before. He was known to me as a competent architect, and he had somewhat of a reputation as an authority on "Germanic" history. I was quite surprised to find in him a friend. He visited me frequently in the evening and always displayed an outright aggressive cheerfulness. Usually he would open the conversation with, "Today I am in a mood to get drunk with you." And that's what inevitably happened. I could only guess at the motive that brought him to me. Many Jews had been taking their own lives, and he may have wanted to act as a buffer where I was concerned.

"These are idiots," he would repeat over and over. "Don't they understand that this scare will pass?" To counter my expressed doubts, the practicing Protestant laid down a characteristic challenge: "Have you lost all faith? God will help!" He became very angry when I replied, "And what will happen until He gets around to it?"

He felt insulted in his religious conviction and pulled out all stops. Had I forgotten the Sermon on the Mount, the blessings? He cited, "Blessed are the humble and oppressed and the unjustly defamed, for they will enter the heavenly kingdom." When he continued that one should be happy and glad about it, I was quite baffled by the turn the conversation was taking. We had been drinking too much.

I rose from the comfortable chair in front of the fireplace, and we made our way, slightly tipsy and with uncertain stride, down to the wine cellar. This was the right place for the uninhibited altercations that can be so much fun between friends. Our roles had been reversed. I did not play the devil's advocate, but I did endeavor to make sense of the ideology of the master race, which saw law, power, and fate on its side, to conquer the world. I was plagued by the question of whether Hitler's followers really believed in the doctrine of racial superiority he had already expounded in *Mein Kampf* and which could now be heard in all official pronouncements and speeches. Could it really be that they believed that the countries East and West were populated by enemies who were a threat to Germany's existence and therefore had to be defeated? Were they really persuaded that "the" Jews were inhumanly evil and "Germany's misfortune"?

"But certainly," said Richard, "they follow the Führer unwaveringly and would do so even if they knew that the Jews make up less than 1 percent of Germany's population, and that more than 25 percent of the scientists who have earned the Nobel Prize for Germany are exactly those despised Jews. They also believe that the theory of relativity can only be a fraud because Albert Einstein is a Jew. The Western countries have offered teaching chairs to the world-renowned physicists, mathematicians, and chemists should they lose their positions because they are Jews. The compositions of Mahler, Mendelssohn, and Schönberg are no longer allowed to be performed; the books of Heine, Kafka, Stefan Zweig, and so many others, which have been translated into all languages of the world, are prohibited in their original tongue.

"Are you familiar with humor of the Berliners?" asked Richard. "You know the Berliners, who love to quote 'Götz von Berlichingen,'* now they say in equally vulgar terms: 'It's impossible to stuff one's self as much as one has to puke.' Max Liebermann supposedly said this when he resigned his seat as president at the Academy of Art."†

When I—somewhat unhappy—began to speak about black sheep among Jews, Richard turned serious: "With talk like that, you show that you are already infected. Why do you expect all Jews to be without fault? A statistic once showed that there are fewer criminals among Jews than among Christians. But isn't this beside the point? What is this supposed to prove? Doesn't every individual have the right to be judged according to personal guilt—or personal merit?" He quoted a passage, unknown to me, which he said was by Heine:

---

*A reference to the play by Goethe of the same name in which the phrase "He may kiss my ass" occurs. The expression "Götz von Berlichingen" is a commonly used code for the more vulgar phrase. (Trans.)

†Max Liebermann was a revered German-Jewish painter and known for his Berlin wit. He died in 1938 in his eighties. His wife committed suicide later as she was about to be deported to a concentration camp.

"If pride in one's birth were not such a foolish contradiction, it would be possible to take pride in being the descendant of martyrs, who gave to the world the one God and a moral code that is the cornerstone of Western civilization."

We spent many a night in animated discussion. I hadn't drunk this much since the war. We had a good time. In spite of everything, yes, we had a good time. But Richard had been observed. His visits with me were sufficient reason for the people of Wesel to ban and isolate him professionally and socially.

After the war, in 1947, I received a letter from Richard Schüren in New York. His two sons had been killed in Russia. Attached to the letter was his detailed blueprint for the rebuilding of Wesel, the German town that had suffered the most extensive damage in the wartime bombings. He thought it only natural that I should have the same interest in this as he did and that maybe—as an American citizen—I might be able to influence the authorities in New York to take a favorable view and maybe even help. After all, he wrote, Peter Minuit, a citizen of Wesel, acquired the land upon which New York was built. I got in touch with Robert Moses, New York City's celebrated commissioner, who was credited with having created the city's most beautiful bridges, beaches, and parks. But in the prevailing postwar climate, my efforts were for naught. Richard Schüren remains one of the rare human beings who, at a time of general misguided judgment, followed his own conscience even in the face of danger to his personal safety.

The Catholic priest told me: "Today we must find the time for a serious discussion. The occasional chats of the past weeks don't do any good for either of us." My Horch (grandfather of the modern Audi) took us quickly into the Diersford Forest. In the quiet of nature, we felt the oppressive atmosphere of the past weeks dissipating. Even a pair of peacefully grazing deer stayed within view in the dense foliage.

"Do you remember," asked the modest priest, who later was to gain fame, "our conversation about Erasmus of Rotterdam and that we were of one mind? But we only spoke about his *Praise of Folly* and his *Lament of Peace*. Now I would be interested to hear your interpretation of Erasmus's remark about Luther, at the time of the conflict, that he did not have the making of a martyr . . . and what he grants himself, he would grant also to others. . . . How can I preach against the decrees of our government, even if they are in contradiction to our Christian concept of ethics?"

I believed then that I did not have the right to exacerbate his honest conflict of conscience, which was the obvious reason he had sought this conversation with me. I asked him, therefore, where the voices were of the bishops and cardinals, which were so desperately awaited by the innocent victims, Jews and Christians alike. Had it not always been the preaching of the Church, from the Pope to the parish priest, that injustice can only triumph if the just remain silent? It was a "cardinal question" that was to plague me for all time: The worst is silence . . .

I believe he understood my suggestion that in this tranquil place we had better consider whether the *Summa Theologica* of Thomas Aquinas still had validity for the contemporary Church. He smiled resignedly: "My concern is about human beings as they are today. I see only few who are really in agreement with the fanatical demands of the party. But many are in a state of emotional intoxication. And for most people, the determining question is what the expedient thing is for them and what will happen to them if they don't go along."

Here again was the controversial dilemma of courage. As a member of a group or community, it is easy to ignore the dictates of one's conscience; the true act of courage would be to refuse to collaborate. But whenever it is a matter of personal decision, there is something shameful: the opposite of courage is not cowardice, but "adapting," going along.

We were living in a time in which it was frighteningly apparent how powerful an effect a hypnotic talent for haranguing can have on the masses of people. Lenin is supposed to have said about Trotsky, "The masses cling to his lips as to the bosom of the revolution." This was certainly true for the Aryan Führer as well, but only a candidate for certain death would have dared make such a comparison.

Today, almost sixty years later, in the course of which I have had the opportunity to become familiar with the mentality and behavior of human beings in many different countries, I believe I understand the resigned wisdom of the priestly judge of men. But I am not the same person today as I was then, and I must allow for such a change in others as well. Only rarely have I met a person who would proudly insist: "I am who I was, and remain who I am." When I was young, the revered German poet Stefan George put in poetic form Darwin's scientific discovery: "To prevail, one must know how to change."

Seven years were to pass before Clemens August Graf von Galen, the bishop of Münster and future cardinal, courageously denounced the flagrant violations of moral and religious law that were being committed in Nazi Germany. But he, too, did not dare mention specifically the persecution of the Jews. Only long after the war, after the mass murder of the Jews, after indescribable suffering was inflicted in many countries and Germany was destroyed, did the world hear the voice of a great Pope raised in denunciation of the Nazi crimes. I am speaking of John XXIII.

What my relatives in a small village had to endure can only be made comprehensible by relating first what they meant to me in my childhood. When my brothers and I were between nine and twelve years old, we often spent our summer vacations on their farm, which was to us like a strange new world. We were allowed to ride horses into the pond, drive down the main street of the village in a wheelbarrow, hold the reins of the horses of the coach—what fun we had, the "students from the big city"! And the entire village seemed like a big, harmonious family.

Our relatives lived in a modest farmhouse that had been in the possession of the family for generations. My uncle was a respected man in the village, for reasons that appeared strange to us: He looked like a Norwegian fisherman and spoke with the authoritative voice of a Prussian sergeant. He was a "superpatriot." Even during the Weimar Republic, he raised only the imperial black-white-red flag at his house rather than the black-red-gold, which was a reminder of the democratic revolution of 1848. The notion of a "Jewish question" would have been absurd to his mind.

But when the new government deprived him of the right to be a German citizen, something must have come loose in the well-ordered clockwork of his brain. One day he suddenly disappeared. Nobody knew where he had gone. Later we learned that he had walked all the

way to Holland to call on his beloved Kaiser, who was living in exile
at Doorn! On his return, he marched into the village singing:

Onward, to battle, for combat we are born!
Onward, to battle, to fight for our land!
To our Kaiser Wilhelm, each one of us is sworn!
To our Kaiser Wilhelm, we give our heart and hand!

Even before he reached his home, he was under arrest. His inter-
rogators, of course, did not believe where he had been. What was
done to him is unknown; he left the prison a broken man. He never
spoke to anybody; he refused to see old friends. Later, he and his
good wife, whom I remember as an ever-cheerful woman, and their
older daughter, who had lost her young man in the war, were first
taken to a so-called "collection station," a kind of ghetto, and then
they were deported to "the East" to an unknown destination. The
official information about them reads "missing."

When I am gone, no one will be left who knows anything about
David, Berta, and Else Leyens.

At the time of the Reichstag fire in 1933, my brother-in-law, Hugo
Herzfeld, who was a patent lawyer in Berlin, lost his life. His sister's
husband, Justice Julius Brodnitz, was inexplicably late for the funeral. The reason for his lateness, as he told me, was that he had been
unexpectedly ordered to appear before Hermann Göring. As chair-
man of the Central Association of German Citizens of the Jewish
Faith, he had been summoned, together with Rabbi Leo Baeck, by
the all-powerful, highest-ranking Nazi Party man and minister president of Prussia. They had been received in the most courteous manner. Göring spoke at great length and with surprising candor. He
declared that after the seizure of power, it had been necessary to give
free rein to the SA troopers. But now the time had come to call them
off. The excesses would soon cease, and law and order would be
restored.

The two Jewish gentlemen were asked to make this declaration
known to the widest possible circles. Most Jews in those days were
only too willing to lend a believing ear to the highest authorities.
Didn't Hitler, when he accepted his nomination as chancellor, swear

an oath to uphold the constitution, which guaranteed Jews their rights as citizens? Article 109 of the constitution guaranteed "equality before the law" for all Germans; article 135 "complete freedom of conscience and of worship" for all residents within the German Reich.

"Hitler won't renege on a solemn oath," people said. "In the end, this fanatical party politician will become a responsible statesman." Nobody saw any reason why he should want to mislead the world. The precarious economic situation had to be brought under control. Berlin was in the midst of preparations for the Olympic Games. The capital of the "new" Germany would give the athletes of the world a brilliant reception. Berlin was the meeting place of diplomats and journalists of the international press. They had to be persuaded of a peaceful rule under the swastika and that there were no violent excesses against the Jews. How much more believable would this assertion be if the declaration were made by prominent Jewish leaders themselves?

In fact, Berlin returned to its normal, bustling activity. No longer were excesses "visible" in the streets. But in smaller towns, the situation grew increasingly worse. The first actions organized by the state, the enactment of exclusionary laws and secret decrees against the Jews, were followed by increasingly terrifying events, which never let up for as long as the Nazi regime lasted: the suicides of desperate Jews. It began with those who did not want to go on living when the new government declared that they no longer were Germans. I remember one case: Dr. Arthur Schlesinger, a renowned Berlin physician, who had been bestowed with honors and medals, committed suicide when SA troopers barred him from entering his own clinic on April 1, 1933.

But unlike the high rate of suicide at the time of the deportations to the concentration camps, such incidents were, at that time, still rare, though no less painful for family and friends. The majority of German Jews still persisted in their belief that their lives in the homeland would soon return to a normal state. To be sure, there was talk of pogroms. But these had always taken place in distant countries, where primitive hordes had been incited to massacre the Jews living in poverty and isolation. Such occurrences were unthinkable in a civilized country like Germany.

Indicative of the climate of confusion and indignation among the

Jews is a letter of February 23, 1933, to the venerated President von Hindenburg by a woman from Berlin named Frieda Friedmann. This letter presents testimony of the almost childlike trust that patriotic Jews, especially those of the petty bourgeoisie, placed in the aging field marshal's sense of justice, his loyalty to the constitution, and his power:

> I was engaged to be married in 1914. My fiancé was killed in frontline combat in 1914. Two of my brothers, Max and Julius Cohn, were killed in frontline combat in 1916 and 1918, respectively. My remaining brother, Willy, came back from the field, blinded in a hail of shrapnel. His sight has been restored to a degree that he can move about in the street without assistance, but his nerves are shot and he cannot be regarded as normal. All this broke my father's heart, and when I see my poor mother, I feel miserable. In 1920 I married a disabled soldier with whom I live in a very unhappy union because of his handicap, so that I have to bear the consequences of the war for the rest of my life. All were decorated with the Iron Cross for service to the fatherland. And now it has come about in our fatherland that pamphlets are being circulated in the streets, demanding 'Juden raus!' [Out with the Jews!]; there are public incitements to pogroms and acts of violence against Jews. We are Jews and did our unreserved duty for the fatherland. Should it not be possible for Your Excellency to bring some relief and to remember what the Jews, too, did for the fatherland? Are these incitements against Jews courage or cowardice when the Jews constitute 1 percent of the 60 million inhabitants in the German state?

The office of the Reich president promptly confirmed receipt of the letter. State Secretary Otto Meißner assured Frau Friedmann that the president had been informed of the tragic fate of her family and that he vigorously disapproved of the anti-Jewish actions and regretted deeply excesses, such as those cited, against Jewish citizens of the Reich. The letter had been made known to the Reich chancellery as well and was presented to Hitler. The marginal notes by the Führer and Reich Chancellor: "The allegations of this woman are lies! It is to be understood that there never was any incitement to a pogrom."[*]

---

[*] I have quoted Frau Friedmann's letter, as well as the remarks by the Reich president and the Reich chancellery, from the book *Die Juden in Deutschland, 1933–1945,* ed. Wolfgang Benz (Munich, 1988).

The trauma of the first years of the Nazi regime seemed to erase the fourteen years of peace that had followed the world war. "The wounds have not healed, even if we escaped without being hurt," confessed the writer Erich Maria Remarque. He spoke for the soldiers of the Western Front. Who will be the spokesman one day for the Jews who survived the Nazi regime? Who will explain why their wounds can never heal?

During those endless nights in the first year of the Nazi regime, when I could find no sleep, I was haunted by the memory of a particular war experience. It was on the Western Front, at the beginning of the spring offensive in 1918. I was reconnoitering a position for two cannons of our infantry-supporting battery. At the edge of a forest, I left my stallion with an advanced medical troop. To avoid having to cross on horseback a field still littered with pockets of enemy soldiers, I took a shortcut through the forest. All was deceptively quiet, as it often is at the moment of a break in battle. After years of stationary warfare, when it was possible to recognize a forest only by tree stumps without branches, I felt happy to be walking through a real living forest with green trees. My happiness was to be short-lived. Suddenly grenades exploded all around me, and shrapnel burst over the area. I believed myself to be running in all directions at the same time. Of course, I lost my way. It got dark, night fell. Not until the early morning hours the next day did I find my way back. My beautiful forest had no more life; the leaves were dying under the gray dust. I found the medical corps again. They had not counted on my return. I rode away. In my pocket I had a small volume of Rilke's *The Song of Love and Death.* How well it captured my mood: "Riding, riding, riding . . . !" A short while later my horse was fatally wounded and collapsed under me. I was more fortunate: injured just enough to be transferred to a home field hospital.

Why did these terrible pictures, forgotten for so many years, reemerge again and again now? Why was the paralyzing feeling of being helpless in the hands of arbitrary, all-powerful forces repeated? Now as then, everything was collapsing around me. But unlike my experience in the peaceful forest, where I unexpectedly came under a hail of fire, more was at stake now than my own life. Friends disappeared. It was not known whether they had managed to find refuge in Holland or whether they had been deported to a concentration

camp. The uncertainty was unsettling, but the reality often sur-
passed the worst expectations. We were still foolish enough to regard
with disdain eminent artists, especially writers, who fled abroad to
avoid arrest. There was a great longing for a few comforting words
about ethical values, about human dignity from them as well as from
Christian leaders. But silence? Such a resigned silence on the part of
those to whom we looked for guidance intensified the fear and
hurled many Jews into deep depression, and eventually the decision
that the only honorable way out was to end their lives. Well-known
names are today connected with the memory of these suicides: Kurt
Tucholsky, Stefan Zweig, Walter Benjamin—all took their own lives.
Some did not take their lives until much later, sometimes even after
emigration to another country. Most of the names of the thousands
whose lives ended this way are largely unknown and belong to a forgotten past.

During the fateful year 1933, when the Nazi Party consolidated its
power, all kinds of boycott measures were employed in Wesel. Customers who entered our department store ran the risk of being pho-
tographed or heckled. Newspapers found they could no longer
accept our advertisements. My response was to publish a weekly
paper with "irresistible" offers, interspersed not with political news
but with entertaining anecdotes from the history of textile manufac-
turing. The distribution of the weekly was great fun for the young
people in the firm. Delivery vans carried stacks of circulars to the
surrounding countryside, to every village; not a single house was left
out. The results were much better than those from advertisements in
the local newspapers. I had a delivery van remodeled to transport
people. It always returned packed with customers, who, after the
long ride, were often greeted with refreshments and could rest in a
room especially prepared for them. In addition, various forms of
entertainment were presented. A permanent fashion show was the
greatest attraction. People understood that something of a battle was
going on between our department store and the organizers of the
boycott, and they followed along with curious pleasure. Once a week
I called a meeting of all employees after business hours to discuss
how to deal with problems that came up along the way and how
improvements could be made.

It was during such a meeting that I made a remark that was potentially a dangerous mistake but that was prompted by the thought that there might be people in my company who accepted the anti-Semitic program of the Nazi Party and still continued to work for me. I told them that during the war I had frequently suffered more from lice and bugs than from enemy fire. I would now suffer in the same way, I explained, if any of my workers were supporters of the Nazi anti-Semitic program. "Please," I said, "do have the decency to resign your position if this is the case. I will gladly give you half a year's salary with my good wishes."

The next morning, a young woman came into my office with an embarrassed, though friendly, expression on her face. She had heard about my speech in the workshop where she was employed. She herself did not belong to the Nazi Party and wanted to stay with the company. But at home there was a lot of politicking every night, and her fiancé was active in the party. She therefore thought it best to accept my offer—but she would make sure that nobody would say anything against me or my family. As she spoke, she was bravely fighting back the tears. I, too, was choking with tears when I shook her hand to say good-bye. Surprisingly, my foolish outburst was not reported and remained without consequences.

But I was plagued by other worrisome thoughts. Here was a clear-thinking, honest, and decent young woman, and I asked myself whether I could see in her the present Germany, and the future.

Twice during this year of upheaval I was summoned to appear in court. In normal times I would have laughed off the absurd accusations brought against me. "Humor means to laugh in spite of everything" is an old German saying. But I would have been ill advised had I not taken these accusations as deadly serious. They may serve as examples of the dangers a Jew was faced with beginning in the first few months of the regime. I thought it possible that traps would be set for me, that I would be "liquidated" (a euphemism for "killed").

In the first case, a young Aryan woman had filed a suit charging me with being the father of her child. However, when she was confronted with me in court, she declared: "But this man I have never seen in my life . . . " As the courtroom erupted in laughter, the charges were immediately dropped and I was allowed to go free.

The second charge against me was more dangerous. The evidence that could convict me of "Rassenschande" (racial defilement) seemed irrefutable. I could not deny that I drove with a young woman in my car to Cologne and came back with her the next day. Would they believe me—and her—that I had given her a ride, at her request, since she knew I was going to Cologne on business? If not, the very least I could expect was to be sent to a concentration camp. Her fiancé's courage saved me. The young man stated under oath that the young woman had spent the night with him.

Both cases proved that the judges in Wesel had not yet been completely intimidated by political directives. Only a year later, Hitler was able to declare, to frenetic applause, that the SS had followed his orders when they murdered the SA chief Ernst Röhm and hundreds of SA men, General Kurt von Schleicher and his wife, and Edgar Jung, the trusted adviser of the previous chancellor, Franz von Papen. All court proceedings were dispensed with. From then on, the administration of "völkisch" [national] justice was in the hands of blind followers of the Führer.

Whether Hitler knew about similar events that took place in communist Russia is not certain. But one episode may be characteristic: Lenin informed Rosa Luxemburg, who in 1919 was murdered by German rightist soldiers, that he authorized the Czekha [precursor of the KGB] to execute eight hundred enemies of the republic. She engaged him in an argument and objected: "We were not brought to our knees by terrorism. What makes you think your terror will accomplish more?" Lenin answered: "We survived only because their terror wasn't powerful enough, not consistent, not repetitive, not constantly intensifying and extending over everyone. We shall not commit such an error. The decisive mistake of past revolutions has not been that too many but rather too few people were executed." Such an "error" would not be repeated under the Führer's regime in Germany either.

Max Stamm of Düsseldorf, my mother's cousin, had lost his only son in World War I. Since then, his wife had been suffering from depression and refused to leave her bed. For fifteen years, the good man returned home every day from work, did the cooking, and sat at her bedside. One evening in 1933, a troop of SA men suddenly appeared for a search, a frequent occurrence then. Herr Stamm was, of course, frightened, and he showed them everything they asked for in his modest apartment. But the old, intimidated man became angry when the uniformed men tried to enter the bedroom of his wife. He blocked their way, refusing to let them in. They beat him to the floor and trampled him under their heavy boots before the very eyes of his wife. He died in the hospital.

When my mother told me this dreadful story, I thought of my cousin, Sally Levenbach of Aachen. He, too, was an only child and had not returned from the Western Front. His parents had placed an announcement in the local newspapers: "He fell on the field of honor. He died for Germany." And they ended the death notice with the words "In proud mourning." Is this Jewish, Christian, Aryan, or does it represent a mosaic of human reactions to the same tragedy? The life of the Stamms had been destroyed. The Levenbachs had the mortal remains of their son transferred from France and laid to rest in a solemn burial in the Heldenfriedhof (cemetery of heroes) in Aachen. This was only a few years before Nazi laws deprived them of their rights as citizens.

One day while I was driving through Hamborn, I saw a diminutive, elderly man trying to remove a hate poster from the display window of his shoe store. Two SA men approached, slowly took out their truncheons, threw the man to the ground, and started beating him. Several people, among them a policeman, looked on from the street corner without interfering. Later I heard that the man was already dead on arrival at the hospital.

Given the circumstances, it may be understandable that my nerves were reaching the breaking point when my car was stopped by a group of SA men. They called out with obvious good cheer: "Uncle Erich, we recognized your car from afar. Please give us a ride to Wesel." They were nice boys, these SA men, who as children had played in our garden. Now they were in an exuberant mood and wouldn't stop telling me about their experiences during the exercises from which they were just coming back.

One late evening, my ever-vigilant chauffeur, Hagedorn, came to me, totally beside himself. He had been ordered to open the gate for a car packed with SS officers, who wished to talk to me. At that moment entered Heinz Temmler, in a black uniform with glittering silver epaulets. He was a relative of Goebbels from Rheydt, and a few years before he had been training in our department store as a volunteer. Unchanged, the same charming young man he had been then, Temmler confessed that he had promised his comrades a good glass of wine on their way through Wesel. Temmler and the other SS officers were on their best behavior and apparently enjoyed themselves greatly. Could it be that it did not occur to a single one of them how absurd, even ludicrous, the whole situation was for me?

During these first years of the Nazi regime, incidents that nobody wanted to believe were nevertheless confirmed again and again. For example, in a neighboring Westphalian town, a municipal civil servant was dismissed without notice and sent to a camp for "reeducation" because he had committed the crime of stopping in the street and wishing a Jewish neighbor a happy sixtieth birthday.

At first such an incident would naturally cause shock among the citizens. Few people understood as yet that we were witnessing an inexorable progression of events. First, there was "only" the social separation of the Jews. Then followed ever more stringent laws that deprived the Jews in unpredictable ways of their human dignity. Countless posters proclaimed and everywhere could be heard the slogans: "The Jews are our misfortune! Judah, bite the dust!" Fanatical hatred became the patriotic creed of the "pure Aryan." This creed was far more dangerous than "the patriotism of fools," as August Bebel, the prominent nineteenth-century labor movement leader, had described anti-Semitism. How could an insignificant individual like me, living in a small town, counteract the poisonous atmosphere that was thus created?

My attempt took the form of organizing what I called the "Contest of Friendliness." The event required thorough preparation, but it worked: the most prominent manufacturers made their best products available, at cost, in appreciation of our business relations going back decades. At my store, we proceeded in like manner during the contest. I ordered "lucky charms," four-leaf clovers of green aluminum. The decorators and painters had a truly artistic surprise for me: in the background of all display windows was the silhouette of a child skipping through the Rhine meadow toward the town of Wesel. Numerous posters with the same motif were displayed in all sales departments. A picture book for children was given away free at the cash registers. It seemed an amusing, playful literary game, but it was not without its deeper meaning: It depicted the little "L & L man" (from the firm's logo) on an adventurous journey through the world and his good cheer and excitement on returning home to his native town.

The success was overwhelming. On the first and second day, the store was filled to bursting. We had more customers than in the best times before the Nazis. The mood was outright festive. All customers fixed the pretty cloverleaf to their garments before leaving the store. And everybody participated in the "Contest of Friendliness."

On the morning of the third day, SA troops stormed the store. They devastated the display windows, removed our pictures, tore down the beautiful, wood-framed posters everywhere, piled them all up in the big square in front of the store, and lit a bonfire. A police officer appeared and asked me to accompany him to the chief of police.

Fortunately, this office was still held by Herr Moebus. He received me in a friendly manner, as was his custom. He explained that, to his great regret, he no longer had the right or the power to intervene in the excesses of the SA. I replied with a straight face that I completely understood the difficulty of his position. Neither one of us mentioned that he had advised me, not long before, that I should always carry a gun in these perilous times. I had replied that I would never shoot at a fellow citizen, regardless of the provocation. Our friendly conversation lasted about an hour. Then I walked back unhindered, past the still-burning bonfire and within easy reach of the heroes singing, "We have the best time of our lives, when Jews' blood drips from our knives."

They had the opportunity to do me harm, but nobody laid a hand on me. As long as I was in Wesel, I never felt I was in personal danger.

The next day, all three newspapers reported in identical words that I had been taken into protective custody for disturbing the peace!

What was the lesson I drew from this defeat? The good neighborliness of the people, so heartening for two short days, could be attributed to the lure of the festive contest as well as the fact that most had known me since my childhood. But I was realistic enough to recognize that they all would submit to the brutal force of the storm troopers because the SA embodied the government.

I decided then to give up the unevenly matched bout. I asked the lawyer Dr. Ernst Herzfeld, brother of my deceased brother-in-law, to initiate negotiations with reputable merchants for taking over the management of the department store. There was no shortage of hyenas, ready to devour the "living corpse." Only a short while before, I had had a bizarre conversation with a high-placed party hack, who had invited himself to my house one late evening. He proposed to take over the firm—without compensation, of course. This was the standard procedure necessary, so he said, for "Aryanizing" a company. But since he was not an expert, I could remain active behind the scenes as adviser. I would draw a confidential salary, as long as circumstances permitted ("sic stantibus rebus"). The proposal was not as far off the mark as I first thought. After all, an old, influential member of the party knew the direction from which the wind was blowing.

The thought of emigrating went totally against my grain, so I decided on establishing double residency, which was still legally possible. Italy was the land of my choice. But it was not the Italy of the tourists, nor Goethe's land "where the lemons bloom." It was the Italy of a time when Goebbels proclaimed, over the radio, the lemon to be "the lewd fruit of the South," when Mussolini no longer wanted "German boots to trample through the museums." But it was before the time when Hitler and Stalin exchanged new year's greetings and assured each other of a friendship sealed with blood. In 1934, communist Russia was still the "Jewish enemy." Years later, however, Hitler told Goebbels that politics knew no principles.

An "educated" German—familiar with Roman history and Latin, enamored of the Italian Renaissance, and suffering from all kinds of illusions about the culture south of the Alps—experiences something of a culture shock when he gets to know the actual people. Just imagine my amazement when the landlady from whom I rented a cheap room in Milan asked me, with obvious sympathy, whether I had always lived among heathens. What she was referring to was the large number of Protestants in Germany. And imagine my surprise when at the opening of a mail-order firm, which had been established at my suggestion, a priest arrived for the dedication. Then there was the time when a lieutenant told me that the Italians could conquer the world if they were as good at the business of war as they were in that of love.

The president of the new firm, Commendatore Umberto Torta, an industrialist, painter, and the mayor of a nearby town, took me to see the director of the post office to bargain for lower postage rates in view of our high volume! This initiative showed me, in an amusing way, how much I still had to learn, besides the language, about the mentality of the people. The request was, of course, refused—but in the course of an hour-long, amicable conversation over espresso and grappa.

These are a few of many episodes I recall, all of which led me to the delightful conclusion that a new world of thought can be understood if one approaches it with a receptive rather than a critical attitude. I found much that was worthy of my grateful admiration. Particularly heartening was the realization that among all levels and classes of Italian society there was an almost complete lack of prejudice. Anti-Semitism was either unknown or was condemned when the situation in Germany came up in conversation. Mussolini, conscious of the Latin ideal of humanism, looked upon the "barbaric Germanic customs" with disdain. He told Emil Ludwig, a popular German author: "It is ironic that not one of the champions of the noble German race corresponds to their own stereotypes of what 'Aryans' are supposed to look like!"

Until 1938, Fascist Italy had no race policy. Only after the startling acquiescence of the Western powers in Hitler's most radical moves was the infamous "Pact of Steel," with its fateful consequences, concluded between the Führer and Il Duce.

In the course of four years of intense, successful business activities, I was received with warmth and friendship everywhere. Italy provided me with something of a healing therapy for the trauma the Nazis' invasion of my life had caused.

In 1935, I had to return to Wesel for a short while to take care of a few matters. I found my mother totally isolated and lonely. So was my sister Grete, who, since the death of her husband, had regarded it as her duty to live with our mother. Not one of the many old "friends" ever paid them a visit. Fortunately, they were not harassed in any way—at least not at that point in time.

On the train ride back to Italy, I was alone in the compartment with a young woman, who soon guessed the reason for my downcast demeanor. She told me that she was a Swiss journalist and was returning to Basel after a stay of a few months in Germany. The conversation was guarded, because I was predisposed to suspect a Nazi spy in any stranger. My distrust grew when she told me about interviews she conducted with high Nazi officials, and especially with members of the SS, which, she said, had changed her whole life. She had visited Germany every year for a decade, had published articles in Swiss newspapers, and had lectured on German music and literature. Now, for the first time, she was not returning with an enthusiastic report about German culture, but with many unanswered questions. She had to ask herself, she said, whether she had been wrong all along and whether what she had uncritically admired as German culture had not always been merely a thin veneer of civilization. Millions of Germans were now persuaded of the superiority of their Aryan race.

One Gauleiter had told her that sixty million Germans—and soon many more—would be forged into an indivisible unit, which would follow *one* leader, while the Western neighbors would be torn apart by battling parties. Then he unleashed a diatribe on the weakness of the "Jewish" democracies. The Jewish question, she said, had become an obsession that overshadowed all normal patterns of thinking. The SS were apparently being trained to discover in brutality and fanaticism important national values. One terrible question inevitably posed itself to her: Were these young men being systematically indoctrinated and hardened to carry out a pogrom? It would be the first since the Middle Ages, she said, but it would be much worse, since it would have the power of the government behind it.

She also spoke with Jews, rabbis and freethinkers, with a few old and many newly converted Zionists, who put their trust in a Jewish state in Palestine, and with those who viewed themselves as good Germans and quoted people like Gabriel Riesser, who had said in 1830: "We did not migrate in; we are born in. Whoever takes my citizenship away from me makes me homeless."

The garrulous journalist apparently sought to cheer me up with some of the stories she had heard from young Jews. Here is an unforgettable one: A rich man gets to heaven. St. Peter says that since he had led a virtuous life, he had earned his place, but only after he had seen the other place. Taken down in the heavenly elevator with the speed of light, he finds a beautiful park: expansive meadows strewn with flower beds, white birches shimmering between dark firs, fountains with rushing water, and beautiful women beckoning him to a richly laid table. He rushes back to heaven on wings of enthusiasm. St. Peter is not surprised about his decision in favor of earthly goods and quickly sends him away again. But now it is all dark down there. Emaciated people groan under heavy burdens. A blazing fire flares in the distance. "Where is my garden of paradise, the one I was in yesterday?" he asks two thugs who fall on him. "Yes, yesterday," one of them says as he is trouncing him. "Yesterday you were a tourist."

I shared the intelligent woman's enjoyment of the moral of the story, although the picture that intruded on my mind was that of penniless emigrants in Italy, a land they knew before only as tourists. Those who know the language will recall Dante's "nessun' maggior dolor"—"No greater pain: the memory of a happy past revives, but here is nothing but misery with no way out."

She said she had discussed these and other stories with a psychoanalyst for whom the meaning seemed clear. All had, she was told, one decisive aspect in common: the desire of the unconscious (as Freud called it) to overcome death or at least a world that seemed a Kafkaesque scenario. In addition, she was told, it was typical of Jewish humor, which had been preserved in spite of everything, to make fun of oneself even in a desperate situation.

It had been difficult for her to keep a straight face during a talk with a Gauleiter, who gave her a bizarre illustration of the Führer's "scientific genius." He would send his personal photographer to important negotiations if he suspected someone of having Jewish blood. Hitler was supposedly able to recognize someone as Aryan or Semitic by the shape of the earlobe. (What I took to be one of many dumb anecdotes circulating could be read about in detail after the war!)

My earlier distrust of the woman had long vanished. We spoke about the problem of intermarriage, which was estimated to be about 50 percent in the larger cities. She mentioned a well-known engineer in Cologne; the name Eduard Behrbalk came up. "My Uncle Eddie," I acknowledged, and I told her the romantic story, which for her was of sociological interest. Eddie, a naval officer during the war, who was tall, blond, and blue-eyed (stereotypically Aryan), fell in love with my Aunt Fanny, who was of small stature, round, and black-haired (stereotypically Semitic). But her parents would not permit the suitor to even set foot in their house. For seven years, so the family story went, Eduard made the three-hour journey on weekends to the village where his unattainable love resided. For seven years his contact with her was limited to nocturnal serenades in front of her house. A "happy ending" was made possible when he, after the required religious studies, converted to Judaism. They were happily married until Fanny's death. Their only son emigrated to Israel, where he is a thriving manufacturer with many children and grandchildren. Eduard visited him after the war. The whole street turned out to greet him with banners in German: "Welcome, Father of our Hannes!" The marriage of Eduard and Fanny may stand as a good example of intermarriages that have taken place for centuries and often produced great generals and eminent scholars.

We were approaching the border. The control on the German side in Basel was cursory. But just as the customs inspector was leaving, he apparently became suspicious and asked whether we belonged together. When we said no, he asked me to step off the train with my luggage. "I'll wait for you at the Swiss station," the lady said in German, using the familiar form of address, *du*, for "you." The officer became angry. "A moment ago you said you didn't know each other. Why are you addressing him in the familiar?" he demanded. The lady replied, "We are quick with that kind of thing." She turned to me and said, "You can count on it, you are expected in Switzerland."

Although I feared the worst, nothing really happened to me personally. My luggage was thoroughly searched, a camera was smashed, and chocolate bars were broken, but the next train took me into Switzerland. And lo and behold, there was my journalist! She assured me that the next day's newspapers would have reported the incident had I been missing. The incident was for me basically no more than a harmless annoyance at a border crossing. In 1935, I did not see in these proceedings the symptoms of a growing disease in the future.

Soon after my return to Milan, I had a discussion with the former minister of agriculture, His Excellency, Senator Silvio Crespi. He listened attentively to my proposal to get a concession for a patented method of keeping raw milk fresh in all temperatures. He concurred with my view that such a method could be of great benefit to Italy. A few days later, he accompanied me on a journey to Germany to attend a demonstration of the usefulness of the method at the municipal dairy plant of Duisburg. From there, we continued on to Amsterdam, where Messrs. Tietz and Wertheim had set up a holding company of patents for which they granted concessions all over the world.

But in Duisburg, we were able to observe only one laboratory trial. "It seems you expect me to teach a baby to walk," Senator Crespi said. Nevertheless, he declared himself willing to collaborate in what might be a protracted and complex process, not without its risks, before it would be ready for industrial use. He would underwrite the costs, on the condition that I participated in the actual development.

Years of intensive work, in a completely new field, greatly helped me adapt to my new life in Italy. I was lucky to have found a guardian angel in the renowned senator, who was able to open doors and to engage coworkers. My first experiments were carried out in the great dairies of Lodi. It was there that I encountered for the first time what I later came to regard as typically Italian: instant enthusiasm for new ideas.

To proceed we needed huge cauldrons, which had to be made to order. For this purpose, we traveled to the iron foundries of Thale in the Harz Mountains in Germany. Setbacks were unavoidable and more frequent than successes, but, amazingly, our work aroused interest in an unexpected quarter.

We were invited to Berlin for discussions at the German ministry of agriculture. I shall never forget the expression of incredulous contempt on Crespi's face in front of a picture that captured his attention in the corridor of the ministry. Under the grotesque caricature of a Jew was a caption that read something like this: "The Jews were vermin until Satan gave them human form. It is a national duty to annihilate them." Crespi said to me: "At home they will believe that I am making a tasteless joke about present-day Germany. But I shall have a serious talk with the king and Ratti about this." (Count Ratti was his son-in-law and the governor of the Vatican.)

Strangely enough, I was filled with a sense of shame that the refined old diplomat should be confronted with such a vulgar picture and malicious text (common in *Der Stürmer,* Streicher's anti-Semitic hate tabloid from Nuremberg) in a German ministerial building. At the same time, I was appalled by my own stupidity that I never took Dietrich Eckart, Hitler's friend and mentor, seriously. He had already called for the total annihilation of the Jews in the 1920s.

When I showed Senator Crespi the famous Zoological Garden, he was amused by a banner between two animal sculptures at the gate, which read: "We follow our Führer!" Crespi remarked, "I can understand the animals. But why human beings?"

During the next few years, my business took me frequently to Kiel, where the dairy research institute of the university examined the results of our efforts. The professors were all aware of my origin, of course, but they showed me the proper courtesy. For them I was the Italian expert of the new method. One Sunday afternoon, back once again in Kiel, I wandered far from the crowd along the beach. Suddenly I caught the eyes of a child, watching me with curiosity. These eyes looked at me from inside a sand castle, and when I waved, a small voice called out "Hello." I was not a little surprised, since the customary greeting in those days was "Heil Hitler" rather than "Hello" or "Grüß Gott." For schoolchildren, especially, the Nazi greeting seemed to have become mandatory.

I walked over to the sand castle, and to my surprise, the child with unkempt hair and angelic face turned out to be a pretty teenage girl of about sixteen. I asked her what school she attended, and she said that she had had to leave school a long time ago because she was Jewish. It had been for the best, she said, for as the only Jewish girl in her class, it had not been easy for her. Now she went to the Kulturbund, the only Jewish organization for literature and culture that was permitted. She was allowed to recite her favorite poems there and sing in a choral group.

Lilly and I soon became friends inasmuch as that is possible between a young girl and a man twice her age. She must have seen in me a kind of substitute father. Only this can explain the stream of emotions with which she declared her feelings, as well as the trust she put in me. She told me that she was living alone with her mother. Her father had been arrested a long time ago and was being held in an unknown place. Lilly delighted in talking to me about her poems. I was deeply touched by her recitations of the poet Goethe: "The future covers pain and delight / step by step before our sight / but fearless we push on . . . ," and finally, with the trusting, devout expression of a child, "We bid you hope."

When I asked her why her family had not left Germany, she said that it was impossible to get visas for any country; besides, they had no money. Yet, in spite the desperate situation, she was not disheartened. She harbored the same illusion that can be found in Anne Frank's diary: "Yes, at the core all human beings are good." She dreamed as only a young girl can dream, able to transform a harsh reality with the power of her imagination. She was totally naive, idealistic, and apolitical.

About a year later, when my business took me back to Kiel, I called Lilly. Her mother answered the telephone. Lilly had been taken away. Her mother did not know where she was being held.

"The Germans love the Italians, but they don't respect them, whereas the Italians respect the Germans, but don't love them." The German professor Karl Richter was a pleasant exception to such vox populi. As scientific adviser of METRA, our holding company in Amsterdam, he visited us from time to time. Outwardly he was a typical German, but he had nothing of the loud-mouthed self-importance of the German tourists who were the laughingstock of Italy. He spoke in an even, slightly reticent tone whether he spoke with the old Excellency Crespi or with one of the workers. His vast education was admired at social gatherings. On such occasions, he was quite easygoing and engaging, even when the conversation leaped from Dante to Giotto, from Renaissance art to Verdi and Puccini. Only when the subject turned to politics, he fell silent. I usually sat next to him to help with overcoming any language difficulties. Only once did he disappoint his host at a party that was given in his honor. A young woman seemed determined to get at the truth of a generally held opinion that German men were seeking erotic adventures in Italy. She spoke a funny, broken German, so that I was not needed. Nevertheless, I could not help but overhear that she offered to remove a spot of red wine from his suit at her place. His answer was charming: "The spot must remain. My wife has to see it when I tell her about this blissful hour I spent with a beautiful Milanese woman." The woman was just as quick on the uptake: "Didn't your Goethe say that the meaning of life is to live?"

Professor Richter was a passionate photographer and appreciated the well-deserved admiration from his Italian friends. Senator Crespi invited him to Milan one weekend when a splendid reception for Il Duce was being prepared in the cathedral square. We had an ideal view from the balcony, and Richter told me that he would send an album of photos from this historic weekend to Crespi.

When Richter returned to Kiel the following Monday, he found himself accused of having taken an expensive Leica camera from the institute. Legal charges were brought against him. Richter took his own life. Only later did we hear that he had been the only professor who had refused to join the Nazi Party. The Leica affair was a convenient excuse to force his dismissal. He was all the more "incriminated" because he was "at the time of national revolution" the active adviser in a company that was under the direction of emigrant Jews.

That same year, in 1937, while I was in Berlin, I paid a visit to Rabbi Dr. Leo Baeck. He was now the president of the Association of German Jews, an organization that soon had to change its name to Association of Jews in Germany and eventually was dissolved altogether. I greatly admired Leo Baeck, a rare human being who combined a scholarly intellect with wisdom and kindness. His books—I had just read *Spirit and Blood*—were world renowned. I had first met him ten years earlier at a gathering of the Philosophical Society organized by Count Hermann von Keyserling in Darmstadt. Dr. Baeck spoke as a Jewish theologian on the same topic as Bishop Otto Dibelius spoke as a Protestant and Ludwig Gogarten as a Catholic. Could it have been only ten years ago that such a different world existed?

Baeck was amused by a story I told him afterward about an incident that took place before he gave his lecture. I was in the company of a young philosopher who was very proud of his own physiognomic studies, based on the theories of Lavater. Self-assured, he told me that he could identify the rabbi immediately—he was unknown to both of us at the time. The philosopher was sure that the rabbi would have what he thought were characteristically Semitic traits. Meanwhile, the one whom the young philosopher pointed out as bearing the unmistakable Semitic traits (the melancholy bent nose, the round brown eyes, the sensitive mouth) was Kuno Graf Hardenberg, scion of one of the oldest aristocratic families in Germany. When I told Count Hardenberg about this nice proof of exact science, he gave the dry answer, "I am honored by the mistake. The noble lineage of the rabbi is presumably older than mine." At that time such an answer was not unusual for a South German aristocrat. But what would have happened had he made the remark during the Nazi regime?

Later, the general high regard and admiration for Leo Baeck was demonstrated from a very different quarter. Heinrich Brüning, the last democratically elected chancellor of the Weimar Republic and a widely respected statesman, wrote about him: "Rabbi Leo Baeck is the only Christian, in the sense of the Sermon on the Mount, whom I have ever met." In 1943, Leo Baeck was deported to Theresienstadt. Was it the hand of providence that saved him? Someone else of the same name was taken to the death camp of Auschwitz.

It was during the summer of 1937 that my business took me to Germany for the last time. At the border, my passport was confiscated. When I arrived in Berlin, I immediately called the Italian ambassador, Bernardo Attolico, whom I knew through Senator Crespi. Attolico promised to contact the Reichsführer SS Heinrich Himmler at once. I waited at my small boardinghouse (hotels, including the one where I usually stayed and which my father had frequented for decades, no longer admitted "Jews or dogs," according to a sign at the entrance). Two days later, I received a call with the order to report to SS headquarters in Prinz-Albrecht-Straße. The address was only too well known—and feared. Rumors abounded about torture chambers in the basement from which no one ever returned. I had no choice but to go. However, I left a request behind that the ambassador should be informed if I did not return within three hours.

The headquarters swarmed with SS men. When I mentioned my name, I was led without delay into a huge office. From behind his desk in the blinding light of the window rose a high-ranking SS officer; he came up to me with a smile. He gave me to understand that the confiscation of my passport had been a regrettable error and that it had been marked with a notice giving me free passage across the borders.

On this visit to Germany, I saw my mother for the last time. I called Senator Crespi from my home in Wesel to inform him of the Italian ambassador's successful intercession on my behalf. A short while later the Gestapo appeared at the door. They had been unable to follow the conversation in Italian and demanded to know what it was all about.

I was surprised by my mother's optimism. Where did she get the strength after all these years of complete isolation, when not one of the many good friends who had enjoyed her hospitality before the Nazi time had the courage to visit the lonely woman? Yet she rejected out of hand my urgent plea to come with me to Milan. Not only, she said, because I had not yet established myself there and was still living from "hand to mouth," but, most of all, because of her unshakable faith that God would not permit this injustice and evil to prevail for long. She found confirmation for her conviction in a letter from our former commander, General von Campe, who wrote to my brother Walter, "The intoxication will soon dissipate and demands will be made that those who perpetrated this suffering and injustice will be held to account." Even when I pointed out that she was quoting a letter that was written in 1933 and that much had happened since, she would not change her mind. My good mother's view of the world was firm and unshakable. She wanted to remain in Wesel, the town where she had been loved and respected, where she had raised five children—and where she could visit her husband's grave.

I found the faithful Hagedorn, who had not been our chauffeur since 1934, at five in the morning next to my car to see me off one last time. I should not go away worrying about my mother, he said. As long as he was there, her safety was assured.

I did not know then that I would never see my mother again when I drove through the beloved, familiar countryside of the lower Rhineland toward Holland. My thoughts were preoccupied with what I had experienced in my hometown during this last visit. I was really "ex," as we used to say when we were young (excommunicated!). Nobody said hello when I walked slowly along the main street; nobody even called me by phone after my long absence. I thought about all those inescapable sufferings: those of the body, which was doomed to decay and dissolution; those caused by overpowering natural forces, which from the beginning of time to its end hold the capacity to destroy everything; and finally, the suffering man causes his fellow man. But is this too inescapable? Wasn't compassion, empathy, an essential part of German culture? Did I observe in these last days a world of emotions transformed? Did the political powers-that-be succeed in turning good human beings into indifferent, callous bystanders to human suffering? Was it possible to see in the behavior of my former fellow citizens proof for the triumph of the Nazi view of the world? Is this the German of the future?

I was despondent, not bitter. But I also knew that I could only meditate in such a cool, detached manner because I was distancing myself from Germany. My thoughts began to wander as I entered the peaceful Dutch countryside. The biblical Song of Songs came to me—what love is, we all know; especially if our love is unrequited.

The pogrom of November 1938 was referred to in general Nazi parlance by the term *Kristallnacht* (Crystal Night), presumably because everywhere store windows, windows of Jewish homes, mirrors, and candelabras were being smashed to pieces. But the euphemism downplayed the severity of the pogrom. Actually, everywhere in Germany, Jewish houses of worship were systematically set on fire, from those of architectural significance in the big cities to the more modest ones in smaller towns. Of course, many Jews were killed or injured, and many were arbitrarily arrested and taken to concentration camps.

After the war, the historian Heinrich Fassbender requested that my sister write down what happened at our house in Wesel. She sent this report to me from London after the war: "Armed men came to our house night after night. They smashed everything that wasn't already in pieces, and forced Mama and me to walk with them from room to room. In the library they tore down your picture and one of them said, 'There it is. Where are you hiding the Frenchman?' I declared forcefully who this was. But one of the SA men placed his pistol against my chest and yelled: 'Shut up, you Jew sow. We know you're hiding foreigners here.' I was so enraged at the insinuation that I yelled back he should go ahead and shoot . . . Another SA man slapped the pistol away. They all filled their pockets with things they thought were valuable, and left the house laughing."

The psychologically interesting part of these events is the sick fantasy of the SA man, who, many years before the outbreak of the war, was looking for hidden enemies everywhere. Was it the frenzy of a pogrom night or the result of a mad propaganda campaign? This man believed he saw the picture of a French spy! What he actually saw was an enlarged photograph of me in 1916 after a parachute landing, which a comrade from my regiment had given to my mother. I was an observer in a balloon when it was hit by enemy aircraft fire and went down in flames. Thanks to the new—and at that time untried—invention of the parachute, I was able to return to the ground unscathed.

On the morning after the pogrom night, my brother Walter, a physician who was now prohibited from practicing medicine, drove from Düsseldorf to Wesel, hoping to take care of our mother. Even before he reached the house, he was placed under arrest and carried off to the concentration camp in Dachau. His wife, who was not Jewish and was able to continue her medical practice, had a brother in a ranking position among the SS. Therefore (or maybe because of the serious wound Walter had sustained in the war), he was released on condition that he leave Germany within a specified time. He was able to comply with the help of a cousin in America, Karl Fromm, who sent him an "affidavit," without which the United States would not grant an immigration visa.

The life of Karl Fromm is not without its general significance. In World War I, he had been a pilot of the first Riesenflugzeug (giant airplane) that flew against England. In the peacetime that followed, he constructed and flew the first glider planes. Yet, this gifted engineer was unable to find employment in Germany. A company in Pennsylvania built a factory for him where he was able to put his inventions into practice. In the process, he accumulated a small fortune and established a flying school as a hobby. When the persecution of the Jews in Germany increased, he was in a position to save relatives by helping them emigrate.

But back to my brother's fate. His wife resisted her family's pressure to divorce him and emigrated with her husband to the United States. Although they were without means at first, they were able to establish themselves, and Walter became a respected physician. Thirty years after his immigration as a refugee, he was honored in his new hometown as "doctor of the year."

My mother had been taken to St. Mary's Hospital in Wesel in lamentable condition after the pogrom in November 1938. She was allowed to stay only a few days, even though in this very same hospital she had once been looked up to as a benefactress. She was eventually able to flee to Holland, though with nothing more than a very small suitcase. Leni, her youngest daughter, had emigrated to Holland three years before and had a work permit. The situation thus looked good. Leni would take good care of her. Like many German Jews, they, too, put their trust in the neutral status of this small country.

The possessions my mother left behind were confiscated by the state. She was deprived of her German citizenship. An official report, obtained later, tells what followed. After the occupation of Holland by the German armed forces, my mother, my sister Leni, her husband, and his mother were deported to the death camp of Auschwitz. My Aunt Elise, my mother's oldest sister, met with the same fate. Although she was ailing and blind, she was dragged from a Jewish home for the aged together with all the other residents. All were murdered, by gas.

❀

Epilogue: Reflections on Power and Fate

For thousands of years, Jews had to accept the fact that their fate depended on the mercy of the ruling political power. Jews had lived for more than 1,500 years in the areas that became the German nation only in 1870. As in other civilized states, they had the good fortune to experience a sense of belonging in the German Weimar Republic. They believed in the indestructibility of the German-Jewish symbiosis, a belief that was destroyed by the Nazi political power.

After the Nazis came to power, the Reichstag, under duress, passed the "enabling law," which gave Hitler "emergency powers" and thus the means to destroy all opposition and to persecute the Jews within his reach. Brutal actions were organized and legalized. The highly respected, incorruptible civil servants as well as the judiciary carried out the new potentate's decrees with unquestioning obedience. Within a span of a mere few years, the Nazis sealed the fate of the German Jews. The German Jewish community came to an end.

The fate of Germany was likewise affected by the Nazi assumption of power. The classical separation of foreign and domestic policy was dissolved. All armed forces took an "oath of obedience unto death" to the Führer rather than the traditional oath of allegiance to the constitution.

During World War I, the power of Field Marshal Hindenburg and General Ludendorff extended over every area of German life. But in September 1918, when the last great offensive ended in failure and defeat became inevitable, the two generals demanded that the foreign minister sue the enemy for an immediate cease-fire and armistice. This demand testifies, in the best military tradition, to their responsibility to prevent more losses that had become senseless. Thus, an orderly retreat of the army was made possible. German soil remained unscathed and was spared a foreign occupation.

In World War II, the no-less-capable field marshals recognized at least three years before the general collapse that victory was impossible. But there was no foreign minister to whom they could have turned; no one in the government was responsible for peace negotiations. There was only one man—the Führer—and for him a separation of politics and war did not exist. He was all powerful; he alone issued orders and directed the war. The power over life and death of a whole people was in his hands alone.

Thus Germany was led into unprecedented destruction and the deepest abyss in its national history. However, at stake was far more than Germany's fate alone. At the end of 1941, the turning point of the war was visible. The invaded Soviet Union had not collapsed as Hitler had predicted. His leading generals realized that their 135 divisions, unprepared for the harsh winter and exhausted, would soon face 328 fresh Russian divisions. By this time, even Hitler realized (as he said to General Alfred Jodl, his close military adviser) that victory could not be achieved anymore.[*] To the foreign minister of Croatia, the Führer—who was born in Austria—remarked that if he perceived that defeat were a possibility, he would not shed any tears for the German people. Nevertheless, he ordered an obviously hopeless war to continue with increased fury, a "total"—ideological—war against the Bolshevik Slavic "subhumans."

It was with gruesome consequences that the generals followed their Führer's command: From 1942 to May 1945, untold millions of human lives were sacrificed. Armies of all the nations united against Nazi Germany and countless civilians lost their lives. These years also saw what Hitler considered his true victory: the Holocaust—the systematically planned, and with all technical means executed, destruction of the helpless Jews of Europe.

Let us remember the philosopher Kierkegaard's words: "Life must be lived forward but can be understood only backward." There is no better example in history for understanding the nature of democracy and dictatorship—and for feeling gratitude to be living in a democratic system of government.

Years after the war, after twelve years of terror and murder, the

[*]See Arno Plack, "Alfred Jodl—Gerhorsam und Verhängnis," in *Hitlers langer Schatten* (Munich, Propyläen Verlag).

world heard a voice from Rome. The great Pope John XXIII said in a stirring prayer: "We now understand that we have been afflicted with blindness for centuries, that we did not recognize the face of our firstborn brother in the Jews. We feel branded by the mark of Cain. Forgive us the curse that we unjustly directed against the Jews. Forgive us that we crucified you for a second time through this curse." And he called the murder of the Jews "six million crucifixions."

The words of the Greek playwright Aeschylus come to mind:

Suffering, unforgettable,
falls drop by drop on our hearts,
Until wisdom reaches us
In our moment of despair,
Through God's mercy and grace.

MEMOIRS OF AN UNKNOWN ACTRESS

Or, I Never Was a Genuine St. Bernard

Lotte Andor

✿

Preface to *Memoirs of an Unknown Actress*

WOLFGANG BENZ

Since much is already known about the darkest sides of life in exile, the author of the following narrative decided to focus on the comical, even the absurd side of her experiences, so she explained in her letter that accompanied *Memoirs of an Unknown Actress*. Originally it was a much shorter text, about half the present length. Lotte Andor read the earlier version in 1987 to a small gathering at the Jewish Community Center in Berlin. Later, thanks to the encouragement and insistence of friends, she expanded her story with more details during a vacation in Canada. It reached its present form in 1989, two years before her death in New York on July 8, 1991.

Lotte Andor was born Lotte Mosbacher before World War I in Bochum and had a sheltered upbringing as the youngest child of a well-situated German-Jewish family. With the charm of modesty, she recalls anecdote upon anecdote about her acting career—in Weimar, Braunschweig, Vienna, Darmstadt, and Berlin—which was abruptly cut short by Hitler's rise to power.

"I was always very lucky in my life when it came to friends," she writes, and the key word of her narrative is *friendship*. Totally alien to her was any of the common vanity of memoirists who engage in name-dropping to gain self-importance. For example, she deleted a passage about her friendship with a prominent philosopher. (She thought she had made fun of him, and since he was no longer alive, it did not seem right to her to print it.) The lack of vanity did not, however, lessen her delight that her story was to appear in print. Sympathy and understanding for others (including the former fellow actress who became the wife of the second most powerful man in Nazi Germany) and a sense of irony about herself were the most important characteristics that helped her in her struggle for survival.

Lotte Andor does not write about disappointments, humiliations, and insults to which she was subjected as a Jewess in Germany and as an emigrant in France, Spain, Czechoslovakia, and the United States. Her goal was to describe the sunny side of life. The conciliatory, warm tone of her retrospective lets through only rarely some of the bitterness about life in exile, the loss of career and status. It is greatly to be wished that *Memoirs of an Unknown Actress* (an actress not so unknown in New York, where she had her last film role in 1989) will find receptive readers.

MEMOIRS OF AN UNKNOWN ACTRESS

My mother was the youngest of Sigmund and Sofie Katzenstein's four daughters. A fifth child and long-hoped-for son was my Uncle Simon. Everybody loved him, although he frequently caused this very proper bourgeois family great pain. I did not see him very often, but I loved him. To my mind he had such a noble face, and besides, he was a "radical"—and that had a tremendous attraction for me, although I was only a child at the time of his greatest "shame." I was told that he was ruined for life since he refused to join in singing the hymn "Hail to the Victor's Laurel, Ruler of the Fatherland" when he was an upperclassman at the local gymnasium [high school]. He was expelled from school and was not allowed to take the graduating exams that would qualify him for the study of law as he had planned. This was a great blow to the family—but, as before, he was still everybody's favorite. And yet, he had a hard life ahead of him. His father had died in a fire at his lumberyard while trying to save one of his employees. My grandmother was not able to support her son. He made a meager living by writing for left-leaning newspapers and the sporadic publication of a radical tract.

But his great moment came when the emperor was driven out of Germany. Simon Katzenstein was elected to the Reichstag, representing the Independent Socialist Party. This party stood somewhat left of the Social Democratic Party but right of the Communist Party. He married soon thereafter and had three children—a luxury he could not have afforded before the revolution. The good times did not last for long, however. Hitler came to power, and Simon and his family fled to Sweden under cover of night, at the invitation of friends. At least he was able to die there in peace after an arduous life.

Mother's oldest sister was a sort of rebel, too, although she led a quite normal life. She and her husband had eight children—all good citizens. But this conscientious mother turned into a fiery defender of out-of-wedlock motherhood, which was then by no means as common as it is today. She, too, left the country in haste when Hitler came to power. At least the city of Frankfurt commemorated her later, after the war, by naming a street for her, the Henriette-Fürth-Straße.

Mother's other sisters were neither unconventional nor revolutionary, but to me they were still unusual in other ways. Aunt Rosa, the older of the two, was an intellectual, so to speak. Even at the age of ninety, she was still reading whenever she found time, but never fiction. I remember that I sent her Bertrand Russell's *History of Western Civilization* for her eighty-ninth birthday. For her ninetieth my sister and I sent her a fine two-sided woolen stole tied together with silk ribbons. For more than twenty years, she had been using a light, warm stole, and we thought she deserved a new one. She was thrilled and said, "Now I would like to live a few years longer so you didn't do this enormous work for nothing." And she added, "You always have such good ideas for presents. Last year, you gave me this interesting book by Bertrand Russell. Just yesterday I looked at the third chapter again. Something in it was not quite clear to me—but now I understand it." She took her reading very seriously.

When Hitler came to power, Aunt Rosa was the first in the family to emigrate to America. The youngest of her six children had been married there years ago and was the founder of a Montessori school in Santa Monica, California. Aunt Rosa helped out in her way. She served the children fruit juices, put them down for their afternoon naps, and the like. The children loved her very much. One of the little ones said it very well: "Omi is very old, but we love her anyway." It was a joy to behold her: snow-white hair framed her sunburned, fine features that resembled an American Indian's. Her daughter would have loved to speak German with her, but she insisted on English. My aunt had learned English in her youth at a boarding school, and although she tried to study to improve it whenever she could, she often produced strange expressions that made us laugh. She took it with good humor, but as a woman of principle, she held to speaking English. When the time of her naturalization came, she devoted herself avidly to the study of American history. On the great day, my husband—as a native-born American, he was a witness—accompanied her, as did my sister and I. We waited and waited—she did not come back out. My husband, Wolfgang, sneaked up to the door of the room where she was being "examined." He reported that Aunt Rosa was engaged in lively conversation with the officer. After a long while, she finally reappeared, looking all downcast. "What is the matter? Didn't you pass?" we asked, alarmed. "Yes, of course, but it was disappointing. He asked me who was the first president, and then he asked me for a recipe for sauerbraten—and for that I studied so hard!" Of course, we couldn't help but laugh.

Aunt Anna, the youngest of my mother's three older sisters, was the most gracious woman I have ever known. She lived in New York with her son, my cousin Theo, and his wife, Grete, and their two boys. Grete stayed with her mother-in-law, my aunt, until she died in New York at the age of ninety-nine.

After the Nazis came to power, Grete's oldest son, who was sixteen then, had been sent to stay with one of Anna's cousins, who had emigrated several years before. The younger son was invited to stay with a friend of Grete's in Canada. The three adults remained behind, in constant fear that they would never see the children again. Theo lost his position. But fate was kind. The same cousin who had taken in the older child issued affidavits for the rest of the family, and this is how they, too, came to America. They settled in New York.

Rosa and Anna longed to see each other again, but the vast American continent separated them for many years, since neither had the money for the trip to the opposite coast. When the financial situation improved, we invited both Anna and Grete to come to California for a visit. Grete stayed with us and Anna with Rosa and her daughter. It was a touching occasion to witness their first reunion. At first they hardly spoke. They simply kept their eyes fixed on each other like lovers. After a while the spell was broken, and they laughed and chatted, Rosa in English and Anna, teasing her sister insistently, in German.

Although they both were at an advanced age, they were still fanatical swimmers. We did not want them to go swimming in the ocean—after all, they were eighty-six and eighty-four then—but, no, it had to be the ocean. Hand in hand they ran into the water. A young woman, who was lying on a big beach towel next to another woman who was sleeping, stared at the old women totally dumbfounded. She woke her neighbor: "Quick, look at what is going into the water!" When we laughed, she said reproachfully, "Where I come from one goes into the grave at that age." Both aunts were highly amused and tossed themselves straight into the high waves—and since they underestimated the force of the surge, they disappeared for a short while. My husband jumped in after them, but before he could reach them, they reappeared, still hand in hand, still laughing with delight. I wish all old people I know had a zest for life as indestructible as theirs, and that in spite of all the hard times they had gone through. They died within two years of each other, both at the age of ninety-nine, irrepressible to the end.

I am sure that my mother, too, would have reached such an advanced age, especially since I don't remember her ever being seriously ill, but she became one of the many victims of Hitler. We implored her in letters, with growing urgency, to leave Germany and join us. But she refused. She tried to calm our anguish with the explanation that the "nation of poets and thinkers" could not be as cruel as we feared. When the situation worsened, she wrote, "I have broken off all contact with my friends so they will not be endangered. I am leading a quiet, somewhat lonely life. But don't worry about me . . . As much as I would like to see you all again, I know America is not for me." My sister Trude and I became ever more concerned about her as many ominous stories and rumors began to reach us. Trude asked Father's brother-in-law, by no means a wealthy man, for help. He had already issued numerous affidavits, including for us, and this time, too, he offered his assistance. We pleaded with Mother to prepare for her immediate departure, regardless of her current view on emigration. Her two sisters wrote at the same time, telling her how well they had already acclimated themselves, and assuring her that she, too, would do the same. Our letters crossed with one of hers in which she implored us to help her to emigrate. She had been torn from the beautiful apartment in Wiesbaden and taken to Frankfurt, where she was placed in a collection camp with many elderly people. After that we heard from her only once more: an exuberant thank-you note acknowledging the receipt of the news about the affidavit. The war began. We lost all contact, and the unimaginable horror ran its course.

Through the Red Cross, we learned in 1944 that my mother had been killed. In spite of intensive inquiries, we were unable to find out whether she died on a transport to a camp or later at a camp, whether she died a "natural" death or whether she was murdered in a gas chamber. In subsequent years, we had only one consolation—if one can use this word—that she at least knew that we wanted to save her and take her to us.

As a young girl, and even later when she was grown up, my mother was very beautiful, the prettiest of the four sisters. She married a physician at a very young age, and they had five children. The first four came in short intervals, one after the other. Then there was a five-and-a-half-year hiatus—and then, in 1903, came I. We lived in the city of Bochum, northwest of Düsseldorf. Although we had a full-time, live-in maid, there was always a lot to do, and, I presume, my sister Trude took a great burden off my mother's shoulders when she claimed me as "her" baby. She had made a wish with the stork for a little sister and had put sugar on the windowsill. She washed and dressed me, took me for walks, and performed other much-appreciated services.

I believe it was not easy for my mother, young as she was, to cope with the fast-growing flock of children. My two sisters probably had to lend a hand with domestic chores. By the time I was born, my mother's life was already less hectic. At least I remember only a beautiful childhood. My brother and sisters were always nice to me. This is quite remarkable considering that I, the latecomer, enjoyed certain privileges the others did not have. Trude told me, for example, that Father, who was served a warm supper (we kept the German custom of having a warm lunch) after a hard day's work, would place me next to him, and when he ate something I liked—steak, for example—I would ask, "Does it taste good, Pappi?" And then Pappi would take me on his lap and, smiling, would put a piece of the delicacy in my mouth. I imagine other children might have been jealous, but not my siblings. They only laughed. Another privilege—at least it was to me—was that I was permitted to light Father's big pipe. It is possible that my older siblings were glad to be relieved of this "privilege," which at one time they may also have seen as such. To light this pipe one had to sit on the floor, where the painted head, which seemed gigantic to me, rested. Father also had a collection of smaller pipes, but it was always a special occasion for me when the aromatic clouds of smoke rose from "my" head. To this day, I have never seen a pipe as long—it reached from my father's mouth to the floor. This may be the reason why this scene retained something of a fairy-tale atmosphere in my mind.

Mother loved all forms of art, be it literature (she was on the board of the Bochum Literary Society), painting, or sculpture. There was nothing that did not interest her. Father was frequently too tired in the evening to go out with her. I was allowed to accompany her sometimes after the older children had left home. We mostly went to concerts. I owe to her my love of music and maybe also my interest in the theater.

However, it was my father who had the greatest influence on my life. I loved him more than anybody. To me he was the wisest and kindest man I knew. I never had occasion to change this opinion. And I was not alone in it. When he had a stroke and had to give up his medical practice, one of his patients, a woman I did not know but who apparently knew me by sight, stopped me in the street and told me with tears in her eyes, "I not only lost a wonderful doctor, I also lost my pastor." I can well imagine that many patients thought of him that way. When he was needed, he was there, even at night after a strenuous day. Maybe the stroke and his fairly early death were due to the incessant exertion.

When I asked him one day what it meant to be a Jew, he said, "Try to be a good person—and you will also be a good Jew." This may sound simple, but it was apparently just the right answer for a small child. From then on I always strove to be a "good Jew." Later I found out that a true Christian was also a good person. And even later still, I learned of a heathen who had challenged the Jewish philosopher Hillel—he lived from 70 B.C.E. to 10 C.E.—to explain the quintessence of Judaism while standing on one leg. Hillel answered, "Don't do to others that you would not have done to yourself. That is all. The rest is commentary." This is not all that different from what my father had said.

When I was thirteen years old, I announced to my parents that I wanted to be an actress. I had seen several wonderful performances at our local theater, which was generally well regarded, and they had left a deep impression on me. At first nobody took my wish seriously. But when I kept insisting, my father decided to have a talk with me. He said, "Almost all young girls dream about an acting career. Promise me that you will stay in school until you have passed the graduating exams, so that you qualify for studies at the university should you decide to. But if you still want to be an actress in five years, I shall help you. That I promise." I was deeply despondent, and for the first time—and the last—I was furious with my father. But, of course, there was nothing I could do against his decree. In later years, I had to admit that his decision had been a wise one: my education often helped me along. Later, as an emigrant in France and then in America, I understood the respective local languages and was able to get on well in them. Unfortunately, almost grotesquely so, once I graduated, he was unable to help me financially, not because he did not want to, but because by then the spiral of currency inflation of the German mark was spinning out of control.

At this point I should also say something about my father's family. We had only a very loose relationship with them—why, I don't know. It was only when I was living in America that I became more closely acquainted with one cousin. His name was Moses Loeb, and he was married to a Catholic woman named Maria Bischof. After their marriage he called himself Max Loeb to please his wife. They were both wonderful people, and we became good friends. Even though we did not see each other very often—they lived in New Jersey—we stayed in contact. It was from him that I first heard about computers, for which he had great enthusiasm. I understood nothing of what he was talking about.

There was one story he told me that I shall never forget. He was in World War I and lost a leg. While he was still in great pain, after having been fitted with a prosthesis, he went on home leave. He was allowed to ride the train in the second-class car and had received sufficient quantities of morphine for the journey. At one stop, a pair of officers entered the car. In the course of their conversation, the subject of "the Jews" came up. Their blatantly anti-Semitic remarks filled Max with such pained disgust and scorn, he struggled out of his seat, threw the morphine out the window, and left the compartment. I asked him why he punished himself like that, now that he had to continue without a painkiller. He told me that he had been in such a despairing mood that he did not want to go on living, and, at the moment, it was not clear to him that the loss of the morphine would not help him end his life.

About my father I should still mention that he had no time to mail out bills (it was customary then to pay by the month), nor could he afford a secretary. Doctors in those days did not command big fees as they do now. Until my sisters were old enough to help him in the office, he had to take care of the record- and bookkeeping himself. That was the reason why he rarely wrote to his children after they left home. I, too, received but few letters from him. He signed them "your friend, Father"—and that he was for as long as he lived: my best friend.

World War I is still vivid in my memory. All three male Mosbachers were on active duty. Father, who was fifty years old then, volunteered as medical chief of staff in Lüttich. Even my youngest brother, who was seventeen, had reported as a volunteer. My oldest brother had been drafted—and within four months, he was dead. My father was already in Lüttich then and was notified first. He then had the terrible task of informing my mother. Both parents never got over the loss. The tragic moment is forever etched into my memory. Hans was a medical student, and my father's hope was that he would take over the practice.

The absurdity of his death was made clear to me once more, about forty years later, when I filed my claim for "restitution" with the German consulate. The official gave me a form to fill out. All living and dead members of the family had to be listed. I wrote truthfully: killed in World War I. The official looked at me and quoted with bitter irony the Kaiser's consolation message to the bereaved in 1914: "The fatherland's gratitude is with you." In my mother's case, the "grateful fatherland" permitted her murder. I have never forgotten the name of the official.

Of course, we, the schoolchildren, were very patriotic at the time of the war. With the exception of my Uncle Simon, the rebel, the whole family was convinced of the justness of Germany's cause in this war. It may have been that, as the years went by, doubts began to creep into the adults' minds, but the children did not know any better. Besides, the war brought several pleasant distractions. Since there was a shortage of food, many children suffered from malnutrition. They were then selected by the school administrators and placed with families in the countryside, where they were cared for and nourished. Fresh fruits and vegetables were still available in rural areas, and many farmers had livestock. I was among those malnourished children and was placed with a Bavarian farmer's family. At first I did not want to go, but my mother assured me that it was important. So I went and I actually had a good time in the country. Plenty of fresh air and food helped me get through the war years in healthy condition.

Upon taking my qualifying exams, as I had promised my father, I went to Berlin and tried out for admission to the Reinhardt School of Acting. After the usual auditions, I was accepted. Life seemed rosy—all my dreams were being fulfilled, or so it seemed. But there was the question of money. The inflation was terrible. At first, my father kept his part of the bargain and sent me money, but by the time it arrived it had lost almost all its value. I could neither live on it nor pay for my studies at the Reinhardt School. Despair reigned everywhere in the country, at least as far as the middle class was concerned. Then an angel came to my aid. My cousin Anna, whom I loved dearly, was married in Holland. She sent a monthly allowance of ten Dutch guilders, which was enough to cover necessities like food, lodging, and bus fare.

Since I could no longer afford the Reinhardt School, I decided to look for a voice teacher. Through a friend I met Professor Daniel, a much-sought-after teacher at the Berlin Music Academy. Among his students were Marlene Dietrich and many other actors and actresses who later gained fame. He accepted me, generously, without charging a fee. He was a demanding but very successful teacher. In addition, I studied several roles I liked on my own so that I had material for auditions.

One day the good professor sent me to a certain theater, where the comedy *When the Young Wine Blooms* by the Norwegian writer Björnson was being staged, with the remark that they needed three "little geese." Marlene Dietrich had already been signed up for a bigger role. I went and got the role. For the next three months, I trotted blissfully every day to the "Theater in the Königgrätzer Straße."

The next step was to find an agent. This was not too difficult, since I could be observed on stage. I found a well-respected gentleman named Mr. Auerbach. One day he sent me for an audition with the director of the Weimar National Theater. I had prepared the roles of Puck in *Midsummer Night's Dream,* of Hedwig in *The Wild Duck,* and of Eleonore in *Easter,* a little-known piece by Strindberg. (I was to act all three roles in the years to come.) Following the audition, the director asked me a few questions. When I told him that I had a nightly engagement, he said, "Really? Then you are not a novice?" I answered with great self-confidence, "Oh, no!" My agent explained to me later that for the first year one is considered a novice. Since I was not aware of these customs, it was not knowingly that I told a lie. At any rate, I was hired for the coming season.

My first role was Puck. Thinking back, I am amazed how little stage fright I had. It seemed natural to me that I should be playing a relatively small role at first. Only a year later, I had much more fear. We performed *Midsummer Night's Dream,* this time for the Schiller Festival. School classes from all over the country came to Weimar, the city of Goethe and Schiller, to see the classics performed. Again, I played the part of Puck. But this time I was much more conscious of the role's difficulties than I had been the previous year.

Among my colleagues was Emmy Sonnemann, a kind person and good actress. When I left Weimar, she gave me her photograph with the inscription, "Don't forget me completely, dear Lotte." The course of world history saw to it that I would not forget her, even if I had wanted to. She married Hermann Göring and became the "mother of the country." I heard later that she tried, with frequent success, to help her Jewish colleagues leave the country. But after a while Göring put a stop to her efforts. I can think of her only with feelings of great sympathy.

In Weimar, I acted in a great variety of roles, large and small. I was Cleopatra in Shaw's *Caesar and Cleopatra;* the next night I was a twelve-year-old boy in a piece called *The Post Office.* The latter was the story of a boy who lies sick in bed, waiting for a letter that a wise old man, who is keeping vigil at his bedside, promises will come. The letter finally arrives, and the boy dies. The wise old man is death, who relieves him of his pain. This highly symbolic drama by the Indian poet Rabindranath Tagore was very impressive. I still remember very clearly the first performance. After the curtain had closed, complete silence reigned in the theater—no applause, not a word spoken. We were absolutely petrified. No one among us had ever experienced anything like this. But, when I left the theater, I saw people in the street gathering around some of my colleagues. Then I, too, was greeted with enthusiastic applause as the other actors were when they left the theater. We were all very moved by this unusual reception.

But we also often got into unwittingly comical situations, as happened during a performance of Heinrich Kleist's *Käthchen von Heilbronn,* in which I played the title character. Kleist is a classical dramatist especially beloved among actors—and feared, because the language is difficult to learn. It happened one day that one of the older actresses had to cancel her performance because of illness. She played the fortune-teller Brigitte. Since it was a matinee, there was little time for locating a replacement. Telephone calls went out to all theaters in the neighboring towns, but nobody was free to take over. Then the director had, he thought, a brilliant idea. It occurred to him that even though I was not on stage at the same time as Brigitte, I might have heard the lines and remembered at least part of them. He knew I was a quick study, and since he did not want to cancel the performance altogether, he asked me to fill in. The mere thought terrified me at first. I looked over the text: two long speeches in which Brigitte predicts Käthchen's future—she would marry Count vom Strahl, who was madly in love with her. I thought it over carefully, but in the end I decided to accept the challenge. And thus it happened that I became Brigitte following one of my longer scenes as Käthchen. I rushed backstage where the dresser and hairdresser were waiting. One threw a black robe over me, covering my dress from top to bottom, the other hid my golden curls under a silver-gray wig, pressed a staff in my hand, and powdered my face chalk-white. By then the time had come to push me out onto the stage. I staggered and delivered my lines with trembling voice—maybe more by way of creating the character than out of fear. When the scene was done, I staggered back, and with equal speed I was relieved of robe and wig, my cheeks were powdered red, and with steady stride I walked onstage for my next Käthchen scene. At the end of the performance, my colleagues greeted me with applause and the director presented me with a bouquet of roses. I was very moved by both gestures.

Another situation was even more comical. Strangely enough, this too happened during a matinee of *Käthchen* at the Schiller Festival. It so happened that the circus was in town at the same time. The great sensation was a lion tamer's act, which was written up in a long article in a local newspaper. The tamer spoke to the lions as if they were human beings, and all in a thick Saxon accent. I never saw him and was not very impressed by this kind of anthropomorphizing, but he met with great success in this little Thuringian town. The night before the *Käthchen* matinee, two friends of mine went to the circus. They were our producer and the actor Otto Graf, who later became very famous in Berlin. Not only was his name Graf [Count], he also played Count Wetter vom Strahl, Käthchen's suitor. I did not go with them since I had to perform that night. Besides, as I said, I was not very interested in animal acts—especially the Saxon kind. The next morning, Peter called to tell me that Graf had to leave the circus in the middle of the performance because one of the lions suddenly raised himself up on his pedestal in front of them—they had front-row seats—and discharged some urgent business. Poor Otto was wet from head to toe and fled the hall amid resounding laughter from the audience. To make matters even more disagreeable, the morning newspaper ran a detailed story publicizing the whole affair in a town where Graf was very well known and very popular. I must admit, I, too, could not help but laugh. I went to see him before the matinee to console him, as I thought. But to my great satisfaction, he did not take the matter very seriously and laughed about it himself. The matinee went on as scheduled. We had come almost to the end of the play, to the point where Käthchen's father solemnly asks her, "Do you want to give your hand to Graf Wetter vom Strahl in marriage?" But what I heard was Graf vom *Löwenstrahl* [lion spray]. Fortunately, at this point, the count embraced the silent girl, and I could press my face into his chest to muffle my laughter. There was resounding laughter, however, from the audience. Many had either witnessed the scene the night before or had read about it in the newspaper. Others probably took this for the original text, while poor Kleist turned in his grave.

While I was in Weimar, the Bauhaus school resided in the town and made frequent presentations on Saturdays. There were performances of student plays fraught with heavy, cryptic symbolism, of dance acts with expressionist stage designs. Best of all, I enjoyed performances of classical and modern music. Each brief presentation was followed by a long dance party. Whenever I was free, or sometimes after my own performance at the theater, I would go to be part of it. Since I was fairly well known in this small town, I also knew most of the Bauhaus people. I danced frequently with the teachers, people like Marcel Breuer, László Moholy-Nagy, and Lionel Feininger, all of whom were to gain great fame later. But what I liked best was to dance with the students my own age. One of them, Paul Citroen, became one of my closest friends. Over the years, we had lost contact, but fate brought us back together in an almost incredible coincidence.

At that time—it must have been about 1928, I believe—my sister Trude had moved to Holland. The inflation in Germany had also spoiled her plans for the future, and she was unable to find employment there. Our cousin Else, sister of my beloved Anna, was also married in Holland. She invited my sister to come to Deventer, where she was living, since she thought the town could use a good orthopedist. Trude followed her advice, and she never regretted it. I visited her and the dear cousins a few times on vacation, and during one of those visits I determined to find Paul Citroen. I had heard that he had moved to Holland, his father's birthplace, but my search was without success. All this was, of course, long before Hitler.

On my return trip, I had to change trains in Arnheim and had the usual five minutes to rush from one platform to the other to make the waiting connecting train. As the train entered the station at Arnheim, I recognized Paul among a group of young people standing on the platform. He carried a huge portfolio. As I got off the train, I called out his name, rushing all the while to catch the other train. Paul turned around and immediately started running after me, down and up the stairs. My train was ready to depart. We had a full two minutes. I jumped into the compartment. Paul stood in front of me, and all he was able to say was: "Quick, give me your address." He wrote it down and, as the train was starting to move, we both yelled: "Good-bye!"

From then on we never lost contact again. He had married a Dutchwoman, and they had two daughters. I, too, had gotten married meanwhile. We had a reunion at long last about eight years later when we emigrated to Holland and stayed for almost a year with the Citroens.

In Weimar, I received a visit one day from a charming young girl of about sixteen. Her parents had insisted—as my father had on the qualifying exams—that she first attend a finishing school for young society girls. But she hated this way of life and wanted to become, as she put it, "either an actress or a female equestrian." Her name was Marianne Hoppe, now known in all of Germany. She married the famous actor Gustav Gründgens, who was memorialized in the novel *Mephisto* by Klaus Mann, which was in turn made into a film by the great Hungarian director Istvan Szabo. Back then in Weimar, I told the little Miss Hoppe that I would not give her acting lessons because I did not believe in her ability. I advised her to take elocution, dance, maybe even acrobatics, and the like. Whether she took my advice or went on to study acting right away, I don't know.

I must admit, I don't know why I did not want to teach her. Over the years, I gave more thought to my profession. I believe that technique can be learned, but not talent. The way I see it, there are two methods or, better, two schools. Novices of the first school begin by reading books about the period, modern or historical, in which the play takes place. They may be studying the politics, the fashion of the time, music, catastrophic events, and the like. From these components they construct their character. Many English and American actors seem to belong to this school. They are personalities, the role is created in their "likeness."

I belong to the other school—possibly because I am not a great personality. I often wonder why I, a bourgeois of a good bourgeois family, wanted so passionately to be an actress. It just happened one day. The works of our great poets haunted me, so to speak—Goethe, Schiller, Lessing, Shakespeare. Yes, Shakespeare. We regard him as one of our own since the masterful Schlegel and Tieck translation of the eighteenth century. Some people even think "our" Shakespeare is better than the original one. That is, of course, absurd. But one shouldn't forget that the language of the translation is closer to us by two hundred years and therefore easier to understand than the original text. I lost myself in these strange worlds, in the unusual characters. I sought to enrich my everyday existence through their fate. And how did this happen? I read a role over and over, until it filled my entire being, in the truest sense of the word. During rehearsals, the role would take complete possession of me. And when the director had some other ideas, I listened and came to an agreement. I must admit, I never ran into difficulties in that respect.

How far my bourgeois existence was separated from my profession could be seen from the fact that nobody—except people who knew me—ever took me for an actress. Quite the contrary. When it leaked out occasionally, the response, to my satisfaction, was always: "What? *You* are an actress? I never would have guessed."

Of course, every actor must decide by himself which school suits him best. To reduce this to a single formula: either you are master of the role or the role will become master over you. Nobody expressed more clearly to which school he belongs than the Italian actor Marcello Mastroianni. In a television interview a few years ago, he was asked how he prepared for a role. First there was a long pause. Then came the answer, hesitantly: "Well, I believe, I don't prepare myself at all. I let the role take me by the hand . . . " And this is exactly my method. I hope Mr. M. will not take umbrage with my confession, should he ever read these lines.

I was very happy during my first year in Weimar, but the second brought problems. The first play was Shaw's *St. Joan*. I had presumed that I would get the part. I was wrong. A young actress, three years my junior (at twenty-two I was already older), got the role. That was a great blow to me. Soon it became known that she was the director's girlfriend. Later I heard that they got married. Now and then, I still got a good part, but they were fewer and farther between than before.

So I decided, in the course of the year, to look around for another theater. My agent went to work immediately and, a short time later, he told me go for an audition to Braunschweig. I got the part, a higher salary, and, most important for me, the promise of good roles. Of course, I also had to take smaller parts, but I did not mind. My debut was as Hedwig in Ibsen's *Wild Duck*, which I had auditioned. It became one of my favorite roles.

Through the Bauhaus, almost all my friends in Weimar were male, while in Braunschweig my friends were almost all young women. Two of them were regular fans, and a third was the daughter of my landlady, who was the widow of the well-known painter E. M. Lilien. I became very close with all three, and we remained friends for life. Hannah Lilien studied medicine in Munich, where she met an extraordinarily gifted physics student. When Hitler came to power, he was incarcerated for political reasons, but, through the help of influential friends, he was later permitted to leave the country. Hannah and Bernhard got married and went to India, she as a physician, he as a physicist. In 1965, he went to Denmark as guest lecturer and subsequently obtained a position with the Bohr Institute. In 1968, he became director of the Danish space research institute. Now he is retired. Hannah and I lost contact for a number of years, but after the war we renewed our friendship and, in 1987, we got together with Anne, my second fan, in Braunschweig. Anne, too, had studied medicine, and although she was not Jewish, she had had a difficult life due to her outspoken opposition to Hitler. She is now in an old-age home in East Germany. My third friend married a mathematician. Since she and her husband came to play a very decisive role in my life, I shall speak of them at the appropriate moment later.

I spent two wonderful years in Braunschweig. I was cast in marvelous roles—Eleonore in Strindberg's *Easter*, Cleopatra in Shaw's *Caesar and Cleopatra*, and many others that were not always easy assignments. I probably would have stayed in Braunschweig had I not received a very good offer—so I thought—that lured me to Vienna. A new director had taken over a fairly small Viennese theater, and he planned to produce classical as well as modern pieces.

The opening production was a play called *The Last Son of London*, which was, so I was told, an "unknown Shakespeare." I played the female lead. The reviews were good, at least for the actors, but not the "unknown Shakespeare." Chekhov's *Three Sisters* followed. I was Irina, the youngest sister. This time the praise was for the play *and* the actors. But the attendance was low. The third play was a harmless piece, though a nice little farce, called *The Girl from a Strange Land*. This time the reviews were brilliant and attendance increased markedly. Then followed a murder mystery, *Alibi*, with the well-known Hungarian actor Oskar Beregi in the lead role. I played the female lead, and for the first time I learned to play a role without inner enthusiasm. It is a very different matter to act in a play that one appreciates over a long period of time—one discovers new treasures all the time—than to deliver clichés night after night. But the audience loved it. Their enthusiasm probably derived from the fact that our little theater had been a cabaret before, and the whole neighborhood was geared toward light entertainment. It is possible that names like Chekhov and Shakespeare had been keeping the audiences away, and only this rather flimsy detective story finally drew them in.

Vienna was a most attractive city with wonderful surroundings, but I just did not feel at home there. I had heard much about the easygoing Viennese, but to my disappointment, I noticed little of it. The little man, the man in the street, frequently appeared unfriendly and unreliable. I am not from Berlin, but, compared to the Viennese, I rather like the man in the street of Berlin. He is sometimes uncouth, but mostly straightforward, and he has a true sense of humor—both qualities I value highly. Of course, even in Vienna I met some charming people. Most important, however, it was in Vienna where I met Victor Palfi, the man I later married. His contract was not renewed at year's end, and we had to separate. He took an engagement with an Austrian provincial theater.

I wanted to dissolve my contract, since I expected the director to produce from then on more "trashy" plays like *Alibi*—and that is what actually happened. The thought was depressing, and so I wrote to my faithful agent and asked him to get me an annulment of my contract for the second year since the working conditions had changed and were no longer as had been promised. He wrote back that this was impossible for him to do, and I would have to fight it out with the "boss." By the way, he continued, a position in my area had just opened up in Darmstadt . . . Darmstadt! One of the best provincial theaters in Germany, under the direction of Carl Ebert.

(He, too, emigrated under Hitler and took over the Glyndbourne Festival in England, and later became director of the film department at the University of California in Los Angeles.)

I gathered all my courage and asked for a talk with my director in Vienna. At first he wouldn't hear of a change. "A contract is a contract," he declared, and I knew the law was on his side. But his wife, who liked me and as an actress herself understood my position, took my side. And since he wished me well, he made the following proposition: Should I not be accepted in Darmstadt, the contract would remain in effect for the second year; should I get in, then I should ask for a ten-month contract and return to Vienna for a two-month engagement. That was a harsh condition, but I had to be satisfied that the boss met my request at all. Maybe he felt bad because initially he had promised me the most wonderful roles, tragic as well as comic.

My hopes for Darmstadt were not very high. But after auditioning, I was actually engaged for ten months. My first role was Jenny in *The Threepenny Opera*. I had hoped for Polly, but that role went to Bessie Hoffert, and rightfully so. She had been in Darmstadt for many years, and besides was an excellent actress. Whenever possible, I watched her from backstage. Years later I sang the role of Mrs. Peachum, Polly's mother, in a concert performance at Carnegie Hall with Lotte Lenya singing Jenny, as always. After Jenny came many wonderful roles, among them Ophelia to Bernhard Minetti's Hamlet.

Professionally I was truly happy in Darmstadt. But while I was there, my father died. My parents had moved to Wiesbaden after his stroke, and I visited them there whenever I had time. I saw him getting weaker, and yet, his death was an almost unbearable loss for me. At the same time, my relationship with Victor had become more serious, and we decided to get married. And so it happened that, for the first time in my life, the theater was not the most important thing to me. At the end of the ten months and a friendly arrangement with the director in Vienna, I moved to Berlin. Victor had taken on the management of the very successful cabaret Tingel-Tangel, owned by his friend Friedrich Hollaender.

Berlin was then [1932] the liveliest city in Germany, if not in Europe: theater, opera, film, concerts vied with each other for the audience's attention. The two of us led a rather quiet life since Victor worked late at night. Even during the day, he was kept busy with solving problems, preparing evening performances, having long telephone calls with Hollaender, listening to actors' complaints, and the like. Besides, we had little money. All in all, I was surprised that I did not miss the theater, but I went to concerts as often as I could afford them. And thus we lived quietly satisfied, until one day Hollaender decided to take a long vacation and handed over the little theater to Victor, who had told him once about his idea of setting up a political cabaret. Even though Hollaender's Tingel-Tangel was known as being political, Victor made plans to engage more contemporary writers. He received positive answers from everyone he approached: Walter Hasenclever, Erich Kästner, Walter Mehring, and many others. I, too, was engaged and did two chansons. I liked especially one with the title "Aschingerbrödel" [a derivative of the German word *Aschenbrödel*, for Cinderella]. Victor's idea was a good one, but the times were bad. For weeks Berlin had been shaken by political disturbances. Erwin Piscator, a well-known socialist writer and theater producer, had been attacked, as well as many others who were by no means radicals but were somehow out of favor with the radical right. Uniformed hordes stormed the theaters; in one instance, hundreds of white mice were set free during a performance, setting off a panic among the audience. Many feared the worst—and the worst did happen: Hitler came to power.

Our first performance was a gigantic success: long-lasting applause, splendid reviews. I remember the moment when Käthe Kühl, a famous Berlin cabaret artist, came backstage after the performance and congratulated us. She embraced me and said in her thick Berlin accent, "Man, now, you've got it made—I promise."

We were exhilarated about the reviews the next morning, but that was the end. We received threatening telephone calls; among other things, we were told the theater would be bombed if we continued. Victor called the police, but his request for protection was not met. There were too many violent attacks against theaters, he was told, and the police were powerless. They advised him to call off the show. We had the distinct impression that they were on the side of the Nazis. It was a difficult decision, but the theater was closed. A month later Hitler became chancellor of the German Reich.

"From now on I am a Jew," declared Victor. This is how it started

. . . or perhaps better: this is how it ended, our beautiful life. At times it was exciting, due to our chosen career in acting, but it was always a happy life. What came next was a life of uncertainties, pain, despair, and yet at times also of unusual joys.

Since many of the darkest chapters of émigré life have already been written, I shall concentrate on the comical, often even absurd, aspects of our life.

That Victor should discover his "Jewishness" was the direct result of Hitler's seizure of power on January 30, 1933, and the events of the weeks that followed. Victor was a half-Jew, in contrast to me—I had two Jewish parents. In our daily life, neither one of us ever felt like a half-Jew, Jew, or non-Jew. But all that was to change now.

Victor was more clear-sighted than I. With the cabaret closed and little chance for finding other employment as Jews, we warmed to the thought that we would have to emigrate. I was not as pessimistic as Victor and, therefore, less inclined to give up our comfortable life in Berlin. But he finally persuaded me, and, as a cautionary measure, I took up stenography and typing at a trade school.

The burning of the Reichstag on February 27, 1933, was our signal. We left the country and chose France as our new "homeland." We had spent several happy days there in 1925 during a visit with Friedrich Hollaender and his wife. The four of us had immediately fallen in love with that country. It was probably naive of us to expect the same gracious welcome now that we were refugees as we did when we were well-to-do tourists. But we were lucky, in a way. The owner of a comfortable hotel on the Boulevard Clichy made us an exceptional offer. We were quartered in a room in the servants' garret, which we could afford. The good man probably frequently looked the other way when he saw us enter the hotel lobby with big paper bags. We bought precooked meals (totally unknown in Germany) and warmed them up upstairs. In this way we tried to stretch the little money we had to the utmost.

My brother had been living in Paris for several years already, but we did not want to ask him for money, especially since he had very little himself. We had to find work. And we succeeded. Thanks to my knowledge of stenography, I got a job as a secretary for German and English correspondence three days a week. That was my base income. But Victor was even luckier. He met a charming young

Frenchman, Bernard, who took an immediate liking to him and offered to teach him film cutting. During Victor's apprenticeship, he was even paid a salary, small but something. We were exhilarated. We became good friends with Bernard and his wife, Laurette. Later we heard from a mutual friend that Bernard died during the war from meningitis. Laurette could not be found. It is possible that she married again and had a different name. We shall never forget either one.

The two years in Paris were, despite all hardship, happy years. Since we both earned money, we looked for an apartment of our own that wouldn't be too expensive. We found one in the rue de la Santé in the working-class district of Paris: a room with a toilet and kitchen, cold water, no elevator, on the seventh floor. Not much luxury, but it was our own "home." I remember the visit of a friend from Berlin who was a stockbroker. He came huffing and puffing up the seven flights of stairs, and when he had caught his breath, he looked around and said, "You don't know how good you have it here. I just came from Switzerland—my clients send me there every few days to put their money in a safe place. They are rightfully afraid to lose it. Some ask me: 'What shall we do? We buried our money in the garden, but we cannot sleep at night for fear that it might be discovered. What shall we do?' People with money have big worries. You have nothing—you need not worry. You are the lucky ones."

Another visitor didn't think we were that lucky. He was a doctor from Berlin whom Victor had called when I ran a high fever and had terrible diarrhea. He, too, huffed and puffed heavily as he ascended the stairs. He wiped the sweat from his brow and decreed in a heavy Berlin accent, "Whether it's poisoning or paratyphoid makes no difference. I'll give you an injection and then you eat nothing but grated apples and take coal tablets, and we shall see." I, too, didn't care what it was—at any rate, I recovered. With considerable trepidation we awaited his bill. But he refused to send one, and when Victor protested, he declared, "That's what I like, living on the seventh floor, cold water, one room, no elevator, and then pride on top of it!" We sent him a box of fine Havana cigars. Honored be his memory!

Our modest but happy life ended abruptly with the Stavisky affair. This episode is presumably completely forgotten today—at least in Germany. A movie, starring Jean-Paul Belmondo, was made about it some years ago (*Stavisky*, 1974). In 1934, all of France was in an uproar. The machinations of this financier toppled the French government, and I, an unknown actress, went down with it.

What happened was this. My *carte d'identité de travail* was a rarity among German refugees. But since we had come to Paris before the great influx of émigrés, it had initially not been difficult to obtain this work permit. Now, with the affair, no more new cards were being issued, nor were old ones renewed. But Bernard had an idea. He had heard of a man who had excellent connections with the authorities and would be able to obtain a new card for 1,000 francs. The sum was beyond our means. My dear brother advanced the money to me, and fate began to run its course. This man, unknown to me, was caught red-handed with my card and presumably others, since he went to the ministry on, of all days, the day of the fall of the government. Proof of my "corrupt" intentions was clearly in the hands of the authorities and . . . I was ordered expelled. A terrible blow for us. Later we heard of refugees who had been expelled for various reasons but simply ignored the "refoulement" and continued to live in France undisturbed until the German occupation. To disobey the order had never occurred to us. We were crushed, but we went on our way and continued our wandering.

The period of grace granted us was spent writing letters and placing telephone calls. The result: Victor would go to England, where a good friend, the widow of Siegfried Jacobsohn, had just moved and suggested that Victor help her get settled. He would lodge with her and even receive a modest recompense. We were only too happy.

My sister Trude in Holland invited me to stay with her until Victor would be in a position to have me follow him to England. Not a bad plan. But there was a catch. And in this case it was a dog, Mrs. Jacobsohn's dog. During her move from Paris to London, Mrs. Jacobsohn had left her charming little dog, "Scottie," in the care of friends, since she did not know how things would work out there. Now, she saw an opportunity to be reunited with the dear animal. Victor obliged her by agreeing to take the dog with him and to hand him over to the Cook agent in Folkstone for quarantining. An enormous correspondence ensued between the dog mother and the adoptive father. Missives arrived almost daily with reminders and admonitions, advice and instructions for the care of the doggie: how often he should be fed, how often taken for a walk, how often brushed, and so on. Victor wrote placating replies to set her mind at ease. After all, it was only a matter of a few hours on the boat. A day before the planned departure, the good Scottie was delivered to us. Victor packed all the letters to make sure he would not forget any of the multitude of directives. Then we parted. In a forward-looking mood, he boarded the ship for England accompanied by the very well-behaved dog. He would never set foot on English soil. For he had not counted on the wedding of the Duke of Kent and the Greek princess Marina. And what, one might ask, did the dog have to do with all that? In the opinion of the British authorities, a lot. Quite a lot.

In order to gain even a remote understanding of this absurd situation, a historical digression is necessary. A few months before the wedding, King Alexander of Yugoslavia and the French Minister Berthou had been assassinated in Marseilles by a Croatian terrorist. Victor had a Czech passport. Although he had been born in Berlin, his father was a Hungarian by birth, and the children had become Czechs through one of those plebiscites that were frequently held then. A Czech? Aren't Czechs "Balkanese" like the Croats? Ergo, a potential regicide! All this was explained to Victor in all earnest after he had been locked up for hours in his cabin. His luggage had been searched and the "damaging" dog letters were found. "But you saw the dog that was handed to the Cook agent," Victor protested. "Of course," the official said with pride, "first you used the word *dog* as a code word for the duke, then you got yourself a dog so that nobody would become suspicious. But we weren't born yesterday." Victor asked to be permitted to speak to Mrs. Jacobsohn. Nothing was granted. He was sent back to France on the same boat.

In the evening, the "regicide" appeared at our door in Holland. We didn't know whether we should laugh or cry. At first tears rolled down my cheeks. But the thought that Victor, with his honest face, could be suspected of such a crime was so grotesque that the three of us finally burst into hysterical laughter.

My sister took us in with love. But it was impossible for three people to live in her small apartment for any length of time, especially since she also used it to give instruction in orthopedics. By chance we heard that our friend from my Weimar days, the painter

Paul Citroen, had a room to let in Amsterdam, and so we moved there. We lived in Amsterdam with the Citroen family—Paul, Lien, and Paulientze, their delightful little daughter—for almost a year.

Although it was a harmonious year, it was also difficult, since we were unable to find work. The government of the Netherlands had just then issued a work prohibition for foreigners. (Otherwise it might have been too easy for us!) All our savings from the time when we both earned money in Paris were soon used up. My dear siblings, although they were not actual refugees from Hitler, did not have much themselves. But they helped out until Victor found work.

A Dutch friend we had known in Berlin had written and produced a film for which he needed a cutter. He was ready to hire Victor for the job. But since he had no work permit and the cost of renting a cutting room was lower in Belgium, our friend decided to cut the film in Ixelles, near Brussels. So we moved to Belgium. The cutting was almost completed when a short circuit in a faulty electric line caused a fire in the cutting room. The whole film was destroyed.

It was also a short circuit in our life. Everyone went back to Holland. We had no choice, even though Victor was not permitted to work there. What now? Paul Citroen said he wouldn't consider himself safe anywhere in the world if he were involved with us because "wherever we went, a catastrophe was bound to break out." And he didn't even know anything about Spain yet—neither did we. But in Spain! . . .

One day we received a letter from our friends Erwin and Edith Scharf from Barcelona. He was engaged there as a film architect and was working on a new film. We wrote him about our plight, and he answered immediately. The film industry in Spain, he said, was just beginning to develop, and he was sure Victor could find work. He had already spoken with the producer of his film, and he was interested. We were leery of "conquering" yet another country, but we could do worse than to go to a place where dear friends were ready to receive us with open arms.

If it seems that we had friends in all strategic places, I must admit that when it comes to friends I am a "St. Bernard." Why a St. Bernard? I didn't even know this dog then. But later when we landed in Hollywood, I met several St. Bernards. While the majority of refugees spoke about their past without fudging the truth, there were some who—consciously or unconsciously—tended to gild their previous circumstances or would boast about imaginary successes in their former lives. This was the origin of the joke in which one émigré dachshund asks another: "Were you also once a St. Bernard?"

As for myself, I never was one. Although I played many wonderful roles in my six-year career with the theater and had some beautiful successes, I had no desire to make myself out to be a St. Bernard. When Leopold Jessner once asked me, on recommendation, to audition for the Berlin State Theater, I surprised him when I politely declined. I knew that as a member of a great and famous theater I would gain in prestige, but I would also have much less opportunity to do actual stage work. And all I wanted to do was act, act, act.

Victor and I went first to Wiesbaden to say good-bye to my mother. She wouldn't hear of emigrating. So with a heavy heart we boarded the train in Frankfurt for Spain. The twelve-year-old son of a cousin cheerfully wished us "a good time in Barcelona!" We actually had a good time in Barcelona, for a few months. The Scharfs had rented a room for us in a pension. It was the fall of 1935, and the weather was very cool. Never in my life did I freeze as much as in "sunny" Spain. Central heating was unknown. The tile floors did not get nearly warm enough from the small stoves. It was much more pleasant outdoors, and we loved walking through the streets, watching the lively, friendly people of this beautiful city. We learned Spanish and were soon able, however haltingly, to converse with the Spaniards. We learned to appreciate them very much.

In the spring of 1936, the film for which Erwin was building the sets was nearing completion. On one of the last days of shooting, he invited us to attend the filming in one of the café decorations he had created. It took place up halfway up Mount Montjuich. The title of the film was *Maria de la O*. It was the story of a count who falls in love with a gypsy dancer when he sees her dancing the flamenco for the first time at the café. We, too, saw there for the first time the very young Carmen Amaya. The director and producer had long been searching for an authentic gypsy girl who could play the role as well as dance. They found her in Carmen. Like many gypsies, she lived in a cave in the environs of Seville. This girl was not actually pretty, but she had a fiery passion and the undisguised haughty pride of the gypsies. She had a strong presence, and she danced with real fire. When she was offered the role, she accepted on condition that her entire family would accompany her to Barcelona. Since a gypsy band was needed for the dance scene, the producer agreed. The whole clan moved into a first-rate hotel that had been selected for the star. But the family members hardly used their own rooms. They sat on the tile floor in Carmen's room and lit a splendid little fire to warm themselves by—until it was discovered and further fireworks prohibited. There were several clashes with the hotel management, but money and a few good words from the producer smoothed things over. He, for his part, had recognized meanwhile that he had made a sensational discovery. We saw the rehearsals and filming that night, and the young dancer enthralled us all. Forgotten was the fact that she was almost ugly, as soon as she began to dance and surrendered her boyish, thin body with fanatical obsession to the throbbing of the flamenco. This went on until three in the morning. When it was done, the gypsies went immediately to their hotel. We waited until Erwin was finished with a discussion, and then we drove in a car to our pension. Along the way, we met the gypsies dancing down the mountain to the beat of the tambourine amid laughter and merriment, while we, the audience, sat exhausted in the car.

The film made Carmen Amaya a star and the best-known flamenco dancer in Europe. Unfortunately, she died young.

Just about this time, disquieting rumors began to make the rounds in Barcelona. It was said that cars were being stopped at random with increasing frequency and their occupants forced to surrender their money. Not infrequently, cars were also "requisitioned," we were told. Nothing of the sort happened to anyone in our circle, so we took the rumors to be exaggerations circulated by the rightist parties who were hostile to the socialist regime. We knew too little about Spanish politics to gain an accurate picture of what was going on. But we, too, felt the general tension.

That spring still lives vividly in my memory. We were happy in Spain and were certain that we had finally found a secure existence. Victor was under contract with Erwin's film company. "That's what you think," so they say in Berlin.

One evening, our friends suggested an excursion to Tibidabo. This mountain is the landmark of Barcelona. Its peak affords a dreamlike view of the city and the sea. We rode up in a little cog-wheel lift. Like the Sugarloaf in Rio de Janeiro, this mountain was topped by a huge figure of Christ with wide-open arms, as if he were blessing the city. We spent a good long while on the ramp next to the station, taking in the enchanting view: the brightly lit city at the edge of the gleaming waters of the Mediterranean, dotted with the bright, glittering lights from fishing boats and larger ships at anchor. We took a leisurely stroll through the market fair that surrounded the Christ figure. Ramshackle booths displayed their cheap wares: fabrics of gaudy color, candy that looked like poison, shoddy toys. The bitter aroma of roasted chestnuts filled the air. We were in an exuberant mood. Like children, we rode the once brilliantly painted wooden horses of a carousel, we soared through the air in boat-shaped swings, and finally we ended in the fun house. We made wild motions in front of the distorted mirrors, which turned us into giants and then let us shrink to dwarfs. Edith began to dance by herself in front of a mirror, singing a popular tune: "Miss, you wanna dance the tango? Tango is the crux of the matter." Her petite figure alternately stretched and shrank into grotesque forms, making us burst into wild laughter.

Suddenly we heard a distant thunder. We looked at each other in surprise. The night was clear and tranquil, and the moon and stars shone brightly in the firmament. There it was again, still quite far away . . . "Seems a storm is brewing," one of the men said. Our exuberant mood had suddenly vanished. Hurriedly we left the booth to get home before the storm. Below us was again the city in all its beauty. Nothing had changed. The night sky was as tranquil as before. But there it was again, the distant growling and blinding strokes of lightening tearing the horizon. But the sky had no part in this storm. It was man-made: Franco's canons sprayed death and destruction among the helpless population. The Spanish Civil War had begun.

The weeks that followed brought much hardship. The newspaper advised people to stay at home, but nothing could keep us from joining the crowd on the Plaza Cataluña, where the whole city turned out. Wild rumors sprang up about priests opening fire on worshipers from their pulpits, workers shooting at priests, and so on. On our walk through the town, we observed several people being arrested by military police. We, too, were stopped several times, but were let go after we showed our passports. Shots were fired intermittently. It was all quite exciting.

Three weeks later Victor's contract was canceled. The film studio was closed. The newborn Spanish film industry died in the cradle.

The four of us huddled together, unwilling to give up our new home so soon. Then a public notice appeared in all the newspapers ordering all foreigners to leave the country. The current government was no longer in a position to safeguard the lives and possessions of its citizens.

What now? We discussed the situation. Erwin, who was well known in his field, decided to go to London to see what he could find there. Edith, meanwhile, would go back to her parents in Vienna, there to await further developments. Erwin actually found a job rather quickly. He cut two movies for the English director Carol Reed. Victor and I went to the Czech embassy, where we were told to take the last ship that was leaving Barcelona within a few days—our last chance to embark on a very uncertain future. Edith was to accompany us as far as Genoa.

The Scharfs lent us the money for the journey. I am often deeply touched to think how supportive they had been, morally and financially. I am sure we would not have weathered the many blows of fate we had to endure had it not been for their steadfast support—and that of so many other friends. Fortunately, in time we were able to make good on our financial debts, but we can never repay them for the debt of gratitude we owe them.

The ship that was to take us to Genoa was a creaky old coffin, a hospital ship, stashed with beds that stuck to the walls of the huge hull like swallows' nests. The stench down there was unbearable. We preferred to go without sleep and weather the journey on deck, although it, too, was unbelievably crowded. We were somewhat puzzled by the large number of nuns among the passengers. This seemed particularly strange since Franco was said to enjoy the support of the Catholic Church.

It was a warm summer night. The air was wonderful, the sea was clear as glass; the polished stars seemed within hand's reach, and the coast was gliding by like a field of dreams. Forgotten was the precarious present, the uncertain future. We drank in every moment of the nocturnal journey. And then another surprise awaited us. When we reached the middle of the sea, the "nuns" suddenly tossed off their habits and out came strong, young men. They embraced each other and laughed with tears in their eyes, happy as children who had pulled off a bad trick. They seemed undisturbed by the gray future that probably—in many cases, actually—lay before them. Then they pulled out guitars and mandolins, and all night they played the wonderful Spanish and Basque folk songs. Some were funny, some were very sad, but not we, who were listening from the deck. An incredible bond of companionship seemed to exist between the young men. This is why this journey remains such a happy memory for me.

In Genoa, we said good-bye to Edith. She took the train to Vienna. We had not yet decided whether we should travel on to our "homeland," that is, Czechoslovakia, since Victor had become Czech by virtue of his Hungarian father (a riddle of world politics!). We were told that we wouldn't need a work permit there and were sure to find something. A Jewish organization gave us the money to continue our journey. We made a stopover in Verona, although we were barely able to keep our eyes open after the sleepless night on the boat. We wandered through the dreamlike town, had coffee in the Grand Square. In front of the beautiful amphitheater, Victor said with profound emotion, "This we owe to our Führer."

In Prague, too, we had good friends. Ludwig Hardt, the well-known recitation artist, had migrated there with his family. We checked into a run-down hotel near Wenceslau Square and then called on him. He did not have much good news to report. The mood in Prague was anti-German. The indigenous Germans and the new arrivals could not fill a hall for his recitations. But he and his family were fortunate in that they had considerable money. They occasionally invited us to dinner, and that was helpful. But on the whole our life was very meager. We soon realized that we were living in a hotel that rented out rooms by the hour. But we were unable to even think of moving since this was the cheapest hotel we had been able to find after a long search. "It might have gone differently, but so it goes."

The hostility toward Germans made it practically impossible to find work in Prague, even though Victor was Czech. But, after all, he spoke only German. Even if we had been able to learn this, for us, difficult language, we would have stood out as Germans because of our accent. Émigrés who had been in the city for a longer period of time found the situation no easier.

Victor tried to write for the newspaper *Prager Tageblatt,* and one of his articles was actually accepted. But life was still hard. Thus, at long last, we decided that all we could do was try to make our way to America, an idea we previously had spurned.

I wrote a note to a brother-in-law of my father's who had been living in New York for a long time. He declared his willingness to take the necessary steps. This time it was not another catastrophe that drove us from our so-called homeland. When we received the news that we had been granted visas, Victor was already in London. He had entered England this time without difficulty, since he had been introduced there as the correspondent for the *Prager Tageblatt* and a few other German-language newspapers published in Czecho-slovakia. He earned an uncertain, meager wage. Later he confessed to me that he often covered long distances on foot—mostly in good English manner, in the rain—so he would not waste what little money he had on the fare for the Underground.

I had stayed behind in Prague because I had a good chance of substituting at the Deutsches Theater if someone should fall ill. Besides, I had founded a cabaret, the Urania, together with a few other actors, and we had met with some success. So I stayed behind alone at the "bordello," chaperoned by the Hardts and a new friend, "Riesi." Hugo Riesenfeld had become part of our circle soon after we arrived in Prague. I don't remember how and where we met him. He spoke fluent German, but with a strong Czech accent. He was an architect and was in love with Prague. He showed us all the most beautiful sites of the town: little crooked corners, hidden courtyards, details on the facades of buildings that we would probably never have noticed and many of which were probably unknown even to the natives. I owe it to him that Prague, among all the cities I came to know, was for me the most beautiful European city. Many years later, when I returned to Prague as a tourist, I still loved it. Though many parts appeared neglected, what I loved in particular was the absence of blinding, lighted advertisements defacing the noble lines of the streets and buildings. I tried to contact Riesi. I looked up his name in the telephone book but did not find it there. I finally found it—and the name of his wife and child—on the wall of the Pinkus Synagogue, among the names of 77,996 martyred Jews, inscribed in the "Book of the Dead."

In March 1937, I left Prague. On the way to London, I visited my brother and his wife in Paris, saw Laurette and Bernard one more time, and went to Wiesbaden to see my mother. I did not know then that I never see her again. I stayed in London for about six weeks. The people and the city were exceptionally pleasant. I really would have liked to settle there, had it not been for the recurrent problem of a work permit. In the United States, we were told, anybody who wanted to work could find work. So off we went to America! I harbored the illusion that I could get back into acting there. For, so I told myself, America is a "melting pot." With all the nationalities that came together there, speaking different variants of English, I was certain my accent would not stand in my way. Never, never had I been more wrong. True, I did get tiny movie parts now and then, but only when they needed someone to play a German. Months and often years went by between jobs, and it soon became clear that it was unlikely that my situation would improve. Some may say, but what about Marlene Dietrich, Charles Boyer, Peter Lorre, and others? They had great careers despite their accents. True. But they were real St. Bernards, and roles were either written especially for them or tailored to them. The movie companies could depend on their names to draw at the box office. The story was told that Charles Boyer, whose wife was American and who himself spoke an almost perfect American English, was asked to turn out his "charming" French accent for certain roles.

We left London in June 1937. Again we had to rely on a Jewish organization to defray the cost of the passage. We made sure to repay that debt as soon as we were able to do so. As we approached New York, a big surprise was in store for us. My friend Lore, with whom I had been close since grade school and had never lost contact despite the fact that she had gone to America in 1931 to get married in New York, suddenly appeared on board. She was a reporter for the German-language newspaper *New Yorker Staatszeitung* and came to interview us. Seeing her again took away many of the mixed feelings we had about having to find our way in an unknown country.

My good uncle and his two daughters welcomed us at the dock. He had rented a room for us for the first week. The temperature in the city was 90 degrees Fahrenheit (35 degrees Celsius). We had never experienced anything like it. The tall buildings breathed the heat like baking ovens. So the first few days were almost unbearable. Then the heat wave slowly abated and it was "only" 30 degrees Celsius. To this day, I have not become accustomed to the humidity and heat in New York, and every summer I flee from the city for as long as possible.

Our landlord offered to extend our stay when the week was up. "No thank you," we said, for we had found an apartment. And what an apartment it was! For three months we had an apartment on Central Park West. It came about this way: A few days after our arrival, we met with a friend, the psychologist Ernst Schachtel, who was a good friend of Erich Fromm. He asked us about our situation, and then he said, "I'll ask my friend if you can live in his apartment while he is on vacation for three months. He might well be glad to have somebody occupy it." It was all arranged in great haste. Dr. Fromm was leaving the next day. We met with him, and he bade us make ourselves at home, feel free to use anything, the radio, gramophone, wine, whatever. He seemed like a fairy godmother to us. We would wish anyone such a gracious benefactor.

Now we had to find work. Lore went into action. She had heard that the German movie theater was in need of a part-time German-speaking cashier. Not much of a job, but it was a job. I was thrilled that I was allowed to work at all. The elegant address became the subject of an interesting exchange during my first day on the job. Of course, I had no Social Security card, and my new boss had me fill out an application. When he saw the fine address, he said impatiently, "Put down where you *live,* not where you *work!*" "That's where I live," I said simply. He looked at me in disbelief. Two lines further down when he read my birthday, 7/28, he said, "Don't you know that there's no crossbar through the 7? How long have you been in this country?" "A week," I said truthfully. "Well, in that case . . ." From then on he always regarded me with distrust. But the woman who owned the movie theater was on my side, and that's what counted.

Victor had a much harder time. Even though he was a real cutter by then, the American film industry had been hit hard by the Depression, and we were told that the unions barred almost all new people and admitted them only for excessive entrance fees. He nevertheless decided to accept an invitation from Friedrich Hollaender to follow him to Hollywood. This old friend said it should be easy for him, with all his contacts, to put Victor in touch with the right people to get work. So after three rent-free months, we had to part again. Victor went to California, and I moved into the Clara de Hirsch Home, a hotel for working women. Although it was quite a step down from the wonderful Fromm apartment, it was decent, cheap, and clean. I worked part time, and in my free time I took a course at a night school. Meanwhile, I waited impatiently for word from Victor that he had found work and that I should come to California. But the news about what was going on out there was not very encouraging. Unemployment in the film industry was rampant in 1937, and to be hired as a greenhorn was not very likely.

Late one night, I was called downstairs. When I entered the lobby I found Victor. He wanted me to go with him to California despite Hollaender's objections. Of course, I didn't refuse, even though our most immediate future gave me cause for grave concern. Most important at the moment was that we were together again.

We did not have enough money for the train, which took three and a half days then, and, besides the tickets, we also needed to eat along the way. It turned out that it would be cheaper to buy a car and take turns at the wheel while driving day and night. At that time, it was still possible to get a used car for a very low price. Ours cost twenty dollars, which we borrowed from our friends, the Friedrichs. Then we had just enough for gas and food. We said good-bye to our friends with heavy hearts. Not knowing what lay ahead, I anticipated the long journey with a good deal of trepidation. Besides, I hadn't driven a car in years, and I had an ominous feeling that I was not up to the adventure. Neither one of us knew the country, nor did we have any financial reserves.

The catastrophe was not long in coming. Victor was asleep in the backseat while I was driving over mountainous terrain in Kentucky. It was raining and the visibility was extremely limited. From the opposite direction, car after car came directly at us, wheels squeaking as they turned the curves at high speed. As we found out later, they

were all going to a football game in the city of Nashville, which we
had just left behind us. I was terribly frightened. The blinding head-
lights confused me, and besides, I was probably worn out from lack
of sleep. I hadn't been in a bed for days. To make a long story short,
as I was trying to avoid one of those oncoming speeding monsters
that had taken the curve too wide, the car slid over the soggy
embankment and a considerable way down a slope. As the forest
workers, who rushed to the scene, explained to the police, the car
turned over and came to a halt upside down. We both suffered from
shock. When we regained consciousness, we found ourselves in the
emergency room of a country doctor in Kentucky. Victor was in
excruciating pain from a broken upper arm; I had terrible feelings of
guilt; and we had no money. I believe that was the absolute nadir of
our emigrant existence.

After a few days' rest, the friendly doctor asked us what we
planned to do. (He greeted us every morning with a cheerful "Hello,
white fox"—or so it sounded to our ears. We could not understand
why we should remind him of white foxes. Only much later, with
greater knowledge of the race question and the southern dialect, we
figured it out: the good man greeted us as "white folks"!) We took
him into our confidence and told him about our desperate situation.
He felt sorry for us—at least so he said—but he was naturally concerned about payment of his fee, and he urged us to think about
how we would pay him for his services.

What I feared more than the plague had to happen again. I had
no choice but to turn to relatives for help. The thought was so
repugnant to me that the doctor offered to write to my mother's
cousin himself and explain the situation. The answer arrived
promptly. The uncle paid the doctor's bill and in addition sent
money for the bus fare to California. A few months later, we repaid
our debt with our first paycheck.

After ten days in his care, the doctor declared us fit for travel. Victor was still in great pain, and during the bus ride his arm swelled to
twice the normal size. Since he did not want under any circumstances to bother Hollaender, who had been against his trip to New
York in the first place, we turned again to a Jewish organization.
Again we were not disappointed. First, we were referred to a very
kind woman, Paula Bernstein, who assisted us with word and deed.

Her daughter Ann (as well as the rest of the family) is still among my closest friends today. She recommended a very good orthopedist, since Victor's arm was beginning to look rather frightful. Dr. Natzler shook his head when he saw it. "Another day and it would have had to be amputated," he said. Victor was equipped with a strange-looking contraption that kept the entire arm at a right angle away from his body. We had never seen such an apparatus, and apparently neither had anyone else. We were stopped by countless people in the street and in the little park in the area where we lived, inquiring about the why, how long, and what then. This questioning was getting to be quite bothersome, though it was probably meant well.

The Jewish organization allotted us a weekly stipend of ten dollars for an indefinite period. It was possible to live on that then, however modestly. Our room was five dollars a week, and the rest covered food and transportation. Any other expense was impossible. The effect of the world economic crisis that followed the financial catastrophe of 1929 was still being felt. Four dozen small tangelos could be had at a certain market for ten cents, a quart of milk was seven cents, four pounds of grapes, ten cents. We were appalled to think of the fruit pickers. How much could they possibly have been earning at prices like these? Later we saw a portrayal of their conditions in the unforgettable film of John Steinbeck's *Grapes of Wrath*.

Our landlady was a friendly old woman with cheeks of bright rouge and bluish curly hair. (At first I took this blue to be a sign of some terrible illness, until I saw more old women in blue and even in violet in the neighborhood.) She greeted us every morning with a triumphant "Another glorious day!" Another glorious day? This drove us almost mad. The days were by no means glorious, they were more grayish to black. In reality, she was right, of course: the sun was always shining, flowers bloomed in brilliant effusion, birds twittered merrily—had we not been in such a downcast situation, we would have agreed with her.

Victor's arm began to heal gradually, and we had to decide what to do next. We had to earn money and had to do it the quickest way possible. Mrs. Bernstein had an idea: we should hire ourselves out as a couple and work as a butler and cook! The pay was good, she said, and we could even put away some savings. To my meek protestation that I knew very little about the culinary arts, she replied calmly:

"Just always say 'yes' when you are asked if you know how to prepare this or that dish. You can read, after all! We'll buy a cookbook, and when you don't understand something, just call me and I'll explain it exactly." And thus began our "double career."

The household in which we found work consisted of a rather youngish couple, a baby, a nanny, and a dog. The latter was again a Scottie, like the fateful little black fellow on the ship to England, but Victor took great pride in walking him. In fact, it was his favorite chore. His other duties included polishing the car, the windows, and the silver, driving the lady of the house shopping, serving at meals, and so on. My job was to cook and clean.

Cooking I learned on the job. At first I was in a constant state of terrible anxiety. I spent most of the break we got after lunch studying the menu that was handed to me in the morning. Generally, I must say, it all went quite well. After all, Mrs. Bernstein was right. I was able to read, and my friendly mistress heaped frequent praise on me. And as the Jewish saying goes, when a fool receives praise, he works harder. Our employers were socially very active and frequently received guests, stirring in me the ambition to present them with a marvelous dinner.

But the day came when the moment of truth arrived. Mrs. W. had asked me during the initial interview whether I knew how to prepare her favorite dish, steamed dumplings. Acting in accordance with the Bernstein law, I immediately said yes. "Goody, goody!" She jumped with joy like a child at Christmas. On the fateful evening, I was to prepare a dessert of steamed dumplings with caramel sauce for ten people. I had never seen, let alone eaten, anything of the sort. To my horror, there was no recipe in the cookbook. Desperate, I called Mrs. Bernstein. She told me that steamed dumplings were a South German specialty, and she would get a recipe from a friend. She duly called back a short while later. Unfortunately, the recipe required yeast. I remember the delicious yeast cakes of my childhood, but I had never worked with yeast. Complicating the situation was the fact that the yeast I knew from Germany was a firm, caky mass, whereas here yeast came only in powder form in small packages. On the positive side, the envelopes had instructions I could follow. Nevertheless, I was such a nervous wreck, I sacrificed my lunch break in order to immerse myself completely in the mysteries of the preparation of steamed dumplings and caramel sauce. The result was a true work of art: I arranged the dumplings symmetrically on a large silver platter, then poured the caramel sauce over them. I had cooked the sauce long and good, and the whole work glistened in brownish splendor. Victor carried the platter with pride into the dining room. Five minutes later he came out bursting with laughter. When he finally got a hold of himself, he told me that the work of art had been greeted with "oohs" and "ahs." Everyone took a dumpling and the company started to eat—that is, attempted to eat. The long-simmering caramel sauce had solidified into pure glass. Not even Scottie's strong teeth could crack it. I was devastated and certain that we would be fired. But there was no question of that. My explanation that I had never worked with American yeast—a totally illogical explanation since it was the sauce that had caused the disaster—was accepted, and the whole incident was tactfully shelved. But never again was I asked to prepare steamed dumplings with caramel sauce.

We remained in this employ for about ten months. I really learned to cook, and as a consequence more and more guests were being invited. I was just not up to such strenuous physical exertion, and one day I collapsed. We gave notice over and against the protest of our employers. Since we had been able to save almost our entire salary—as Mrs. Bernstein had predicted—we now had enough to afford a little bungalow with a pretty little garden. Victor took a job as a Fuller brush man. This seemed, at the time, for many people who could not find work in their own field—and not only immigrants—a last, but profitable, resort. The Fuller Company produced excellent household brushes of all kinds, which were sold by representatives from door to door. Victor was so successful, he was awarded first prize for Thanksgiving: a huge turkey. We invited our friends to a feast and still had leftovers for days. But this new "profession" was very demeaning for Victor. He would rather be a butler, and when he heard that Eddie Cantor was looking for a second butler, he applied and got the job. As "second" he was allowed to live in the house. I myself spent most of the first weeks stretched out on the sofa. The doctor had prescribed complete rest. A few times I received a visit from the daughter of our landlady, an elderly woman with extremely English aristocratic airs and politically radical views.

(I have had occasion to observe this combination in several other people.) From time to time, friends would drop by to see how I was doing.

One day I had a memorable visitor: an elegant young man called with a basket of wonderful delicacies. There was a special story connected with this kind, good-looking, young man. He was a very popular guest at the house of our previous employers, and his name happened to be the same as my maiden name. From my uncle in New York I learned that this was not as strange as it seemed. He actually was a distant relative, that is, we were related several times removed. But I did not reveal my identity so he would not be embarrassed in front of his friends. Meanwhile, he had apparently heard about this connection himself from some other source. But this was not the reason he came to me that day; rather, he wanted to make a confession. To my utter surprise, this friendly, well-mannered, though toward us servants condescendingly courteous, man appeared humble and contrite. He confessed to having intrigued against us, that he had told our employers that we were not really Jewish immigrants. We neither looked Jewish (nostra culpa, nostra maxima culpa), nor did we speak English like other Germans (we owed this to our England-educated teachers whose lightly British accent we had absorbed—by now it has completely faded), nor did we speak like servants. His conclusion that we must be Nazi spies had, however, been rejected by our employers, who stood firmly by us and refused to dismiss us from their employ—maybe because they asked themselves what there was to spy about in the household of the lawyer of an oil company. The young man said he now knew that we were Jews, and he was asking our forgiveness. This was once again one of those situations in which it was hard to decide whether one should cry or laugh. Of course, I laughed. This elegant man was so relieved that he bent over the cook's red, roughened hands and kissed them, as Marlitt* might have described this strange scene. He called a few more times, but he never came back. That was quite all right, for I don't think we would have found much in common.

Victor did not stay long with Eddie Cantor. Since he found it simply impossible to find work in the film industry, he tried the the-

---

*The nineteenth-century German Danielle Steele (Trans.).

ater. One day he had the idea of putting together a revue he called "Horrorscope." Horror stories were not quite all the rage as they are now, but Victor actually found a sponsor and a writer who were both willing to contribute, each in his own way, to the show. Even Friedrich Hollaender wrote a sketch for two people and called it "Moonlight Sonata." And since I had completely recovered by then, I played the woman and an actor we knew played the man. The set was designed by a talented young Dutch painter who had been recommended by Paul Citroen. We became good friends with him and his charming young wife—that is, I became friends with her; Victor fell in love with her. Though it was understandable, it was no less painful for me. Eventually the other couple divorced, and Victor and the woman got married. "Horrorscope" became something of a horror story for me—but Victor and I remained friends until his death.

In 1939 I had an opportunity to act in a German play, and this is where I met Wolfgang Zilzer, an authentic St. Bernard. His name was familiar to me from many German movies. In America he changed his name to Paul Andor because Wolfgang Zilzer was too much of a tongue twister for Americans. We became good friends, and in 1943 we got married. The story of our wedding had, like all my stories, a strange aspect.

I was working for friends of Erwin Scharf, the Metzners, at the time. He was a well-known German set designer and, I believe, even a genuine St. Bernard. She was a talented craftswoman. They, too, had had to retrain. Grace Metzner designed decorations, brooches, and the like in transparent Lucite, which was a new material coming into use. Mr. Metzner pressed out the forms with a machine, which, I believe, he also designed. It was a small but successful production. I was their only employee. My job was to take care of the correspondence, pack orders, take them to the post office, and write out invoices; in sum, I did everything a girl Friday does. Since the two were very sweet, I actually enjoyed my work.

Wolfgang had proposed several times that we should get married, but I could not bring myself to take the plunge. The breakup of my first marriage may have made me cautious. Then the war came. We immigrants, refugees from Nazism, became overnight, absurdly enough, "hostile foreigners." We had to register with the police and had to observe a 7 P.M. curfew. This was by no means a tragedy, but

it was sometimes boring. Wolfgang took the opportunity to persuade me that my only salvation was in marrying him. I would
become naturalized much sooner since he was, to my surprise, an
American citizen. He apparently had been born in Cincinnati,
Ohio, while his father, a famous actor, was on an American tour. At
the age of four, he moved with his father to Germany, where he grew
up and became a famous German actor. In 1931, he had an engagement as synchronizer in the United States but did not stay then. It
was only in 1937 that he finally settled there.

It was December 1942 and the busiest time for the little Lucite
workshop. I thought it would be inconsiderate to take half a day off
to get married. I promised to "absolve" it after the holidays. But
Wolfgang got behind the Metzners, and they said, "Nonsense, you
two get married. And without delay!" We took the required blood
tests, filled out the required papers, and chose the next day for the
transaction. We lived far out in the Hollywood hills then and had
two old cars, one a museum piece, a Model-T Ford more than ten
years old. We descended on Los Angeles City Hall from different
directions, a drive of an hour and a half for each of us. We met, filled
out the marriage license, and handed it to the woman behind the
counter, who had us sign it in front of her. Then she took the paper
and continued her work. "Is that all"? Wolfgang asked, baffled.
"That's all," she smiled. "Congratulations." We shook hands and
congratulated each other. Then Wolfgang got into his car and I into
mine; he drove back to the hills, I to the Metzners.

That evening, my sister and her husband joined us for the wedding feast; I believe it was meat loaf. Everything seemed to work out
splendidly. I wrote to the Department of the Interior that I was now
married to an American citizen and requested to be naturalized soon.

A few months later during a visit from friends, the Barriers, we
mentioned in passing that we were married. "What?" Ernestine cried
out indignantly. "You got married and did not ask us to be witnesses?" "Don't get excited, Ernestine," I said calmly, "we didn't need
any." They were dumbstruck. "What? No witnesses? That's unheard
of! Let us see your marriage license." We took it out, and they
checked it carefully. Then they pointed triumphantly to where it
said, "Valid only when sworn to before a Justice of the Peace before
witnesses." We had never looked closely at the piece of paper, and we

had taken the woman's remark, "That's all," literally. We laughed for a long time and then made another appointment. The four of us would go to City Hall on April 2. And so the Barriers still got to witness our marriage. After the ceremony we drank champagne to the health of the "newlyweds." Then our friends got into their car and went home, Wolfgang in his headed toward the hills, and I took my Model-T to the Metzners.

The embarrassing part of the whole thing was that I had to write a new letter, something to the effect of: "Dear Mr. Secretary, kindly forgive me but I was in error to assume that I was already married. Enclosed please find a new application." I was a bit uneasy at the thought that he would think that I had been living in sin, and I even feared that there could be complications on grounds of moral turpitude. But I was duly naturalized, and on September 24, 1943, I became an American citizen. My émigré days were over at long last.

During all those turbulent times, Victor had often tried to console me with the assurance that one day we would look back and laugh about all the absurdities that had happened to us. I am glad I lived long enough to arrive at that attitude. Back then I was often ready to despair. But what were all these difficulties compared to the suffering of those who were deported and murdered? My mother was not the only victim of the Nazis among people we knew. After the war we learned that twelve family members from Holland had perished—five adults and seven children, close and distant relatives. Among them was my beloved cousin Anna, who had made it possible for me to become an actress. Years later, we heard indirectly from Dutch survivors that Anna had been shot on the way to a camp because she tried to give courage to her fellows with impassioned exhortations that the immortal spirit would overcome all cruelty.

I don't know if the story is true, but it could well be. Dear Anna was always a practical idealist. She had been one of the first disciples of Maria Montessori and had established a Montessori nursery in Holland, which then grew into a full-fledged elementary school. Today this school is called Anna-Adelaar-Montessori School—a beautiful memorial tribute to her dedication.

Wolfgang's mother was Aryan, and after her death his father married another Aryan woman. We remained in contact with them until the war broke out. Until then they seemed to be safe. After the war, when communication was again possible, Wolfgang received a letter from his stepmother saying that his father had died. Under what circumstances he passed away, we will never know. She answered Wolfgang's inquiries only vaguely and evasively. When he invited her to come to America, she accepted enthusiastically and promised to tell everything then. It took some time to get all the papers together, but finally the date for her arrival was set. We even moved to a larger apartment so she could have a room of her own. But a day before the ship was to land, we received a telegram from the German embassy saying that Mrs. Zilzer had suddenly passed away. We can only guess what terrible times the woman must have lived through. When relief finally came, it was too much for her and she just collapsed. Thus, even though she was not Jewish, she, too, became a victim of Nazism.

Wolfgang brought a great treasure with him into our marriage: a married couple who were both singers and who were his best friends. I "adopted" them right away. Meta made my life easier in so many ways through her generosity and friendship—I can even say love—with her levelheaded advice and her wonderful sense of humor. I once called her jokingly in the presence of another woman my "bosom friend"—an expression I had always found droll. But the woman quite seriously said, "I thought Lore was your bosom friend!" The only right answer to that was that I had, after all, two bosoms and therefore could have two bosom friends. And this is how it will be . . .

When Wolfgang played Firs in Chekhov's *Cherry Orchard* at the Cincinnati Playhouse in 1980, he found the original announcement of his birth in an old newspaper. His father had worked on several occasions in Germany with Ernst Lubitsch, who had gained fame in his younger years for his portrayals of old men. When Wolfgang decided to emigrate to the United States, his father gave him a letter for Lubitsch, who was by then a famous director, asking him if he could help his son. Lubitsch engaged him in two small roles. For Wolfgang, too, the accent was an obstacle. Later, when he spoke English almost without an accent, he obtained bigger roles, but Lubitsch was dead by then.

Through Wolfgang I got a small part in the film *Confessions of a Nazi Spy,* one of the first—if not *the* first—of the anti-Nazi films. Other small parts followed now and then in the course of my six-year stay in Hollywood. Only once was I cast in a larger role, which was again shortened due to an accident. I played a Norwegian farmer's wife who hides an Allied officer in her potato cart and saves his life. It was in one of the popular "Lassie" films. We filmed on location in the Grand Teton National Park. We were put up at a quite decent hotel in Jackson Hole. I have fond memories of this job because it was all so new to me: the truly grandiose Tetons, the gently trembling aspen, the magnificently blue Lake Jenny at the foot of the snowcapped mountains, and everywhere meadows strewn with spring flowers—the natural beauty all around was simply overwhelming. Our Norwegian adviser told us that this landscape resembled his homeland in a surprising way.

But there were also other, more mundane, impressions—for example, the cowboys with shining boots, which I saw for the first time in the flesh. They carried their saddles around with them, one more lavish than the next and probably worth a small fortune. When we came downstairs at six o'clock in the morning, they were already engaged in a card game with the local sheriff and smashed their cards thunderously on the table. They played with silver dollars—apparently they did not trust Uncle Sam's paper issue. Some had a whole pile of silver pieces stacked in front of them, others had only three or four. As soon as we entered, the sheriff rose and joined our company. He had been charged with staying close to us and keeping an eye on everything. I have no idea when and where he slept.

According to the script, I was to drive my cart, piled high with potatoes, down a rough road toward the village. The freight was precious: the Allied officer was hidden under it, so he would not fall into the hands of the Nazis. We rehearsed the scene a few times on the spot. Then I mounted the coachman's seat, took the reins into my hands, and the horse trotted down the hilly road. At the point where the road took a dangerously steep downturn, I had to cede my place to a double. I confess, I tried to protest to the director, but he wouldn't hear of it. We rehearsed once, and the second time I dismounted obediently at the appointed spot. I tiptoed down to where the camera was situated and where everybody was keeping an attentive watch on the carriage ride. Suddenly there was a general outcry: the horse stumbled and fell down, and the cart turned over and buried the young woman and the horse under the load of potatoes. I stood motionless, frightened to death, while the crew rushed to the scene of the accident. The woman was freed, and she assured everybody, laughing, that she was unhurt and everything was all right. The poor horse, however, had received some injury. "You see," the director said to me, "she knows how to fall. If you had been in her place, you might have broken every bone in your body—or you might have gotten killed." I recognized that he was right and gratefully embraced my double, feeling that I had been very lucky. But that was also the end for me. The cameraman had filmed all the excitement, and this gripping scene was incorporated into the film. The rest of my part was simply cut. I received my full pay, but that was all. Good-bye, Grand Tetons!

After six years, I had had enough of Hollywood, even though our life was rather comfortable there: friends, a pretty house in the Hollywood hills, pleasant climate, and now and then work in anti-Nazi films. It was this "now and then" that drove me to distraction. I would work a day or two, rarely three, and then sit around for months taking an undeserved vacation. Most of all, I had a great longing for the theater.

At this time, I was in contact with Joan Crawford. I had a small part in one of her films, one of those one-day engagements, in which I played a "Nazisse," as we called the female Nazis. A short time after, I received a similar part in her film *Above Suspicion* (1943). The production assistant, Jules Dassin, who later became a director, told me that Miss Crawford had requested me for the part. She later told me herself that she had seen me in two short films by Fred Zimmermann, in which I played some more substantial parts, and that she had great admiration for me. At the end of the day, she invited me to her house for the first time. This was repeated about five or six times. (The author of *Mommy Dearest* was then still a delightful young girl who greeted me with a deep curtsy.) When I told Joan—she insisted that I call her by her first name—that I had decided to try my luck in New York, she immediately offered to write a letter of recommendation to her friend, the producer Golden. The letter worked: Shortly after my arrival in New York, I had a small part in the play *A Place of Her Own* onstage. After several tryouts in the provinces, it opened in a theater on Broadway, but, unfortunately, it closed after only a week.

While I was impatiently waiting for other roles, I had to find work of some sort. I was a temporary replacement for a housekeeper, a nanny, a secretary, and the like. One day I heard in the office of my union about the Equity Library Theater. It was, in my opinion, a most worthwhile institution, financed by "my" producer, Mr. Golden. The purpose was to give actors, especially young ones, an opportunity to be "discovered" by an agent. Mr. Golden invested seventy-five dollars in each production. Nobody received a stipend, the library made the room available, and the modest sum was used for self-made props.

I heard then—it was about 1946—that the well-known piece *Girls in Uniform* was slated to be produced. I auditioned for the small, but good, role of the Russian ballet mistress, and I was lucky. Not only did I get the part, but it was also the beginning of a friendship with the young director Frank Gregory. He was not only a talented artist but also an unusually knowledgeable and refined human being. The piece was successful. (A short while after, Frank left New York for Europe, where he stayed in Italy and other European cities. Again we lost contact for some time, but were brought together again much later through sheer accident.) The first performance was so successful that there was even talk of moving the production to Broadway. But it so happened that another piece with a lesbian theme had just been produced and had received very negative reviews. So it was feared that another play with similar characters was sure to fail. At least it became the springboard for two young actresses: Mary James and Elizabeth Wilson. Mary died tragically while still young, but Elizabeth still appears quite frequently.

After some time—to me it seemed a *very* long time—I received a call from the producers of Maxwell Anderson's *Joan of Lorraine,* in which Ingrid Bergman was to play the title role. I got the role of the mother, who had one important scene. She foresees the future of her daughter in a dream: she will lead her followers to victory over the English invaders and march to Rheims for the king's coronation. I was very happy to be cast at last in a real theatrical role.

The premiere was to be in Washington, D.C. Unfortunately, difficulties arose. The planned theater admitted no blacks. When Ingrid Bergman heard of it, she refused to appear there. That was then an audacious position to take. All in all, she was a quite remarkable woman, extremely gracious, but also very direct if she disagreed with someone on a point. I greatly admired her character, aside from the fact that I had the highest regard for her as an actress.

When the play finally had its premiere, my luck ran out. The role of the mother was cut, and I must admit, rightfully so. For as a friend of the author explained to him, she reveals at the very beginning the course of the entire action. For the second time, I was completely devastated. If this is what it meant to be an actress in America, then I simply could not afford to be in that profession—to say nothing of the mental anguish.

Wolfgang, too, had left Hollywood in the meantime. He had made a good living there as long as anti-Nazi films were being produced. But that time was over, and, like me, he had had enough of the long periods of waiting for work. It would be better if we at least waited together. With the help of a friend, we found an apartment in New York. That was as difficult then as it is today—just not quite as terribly expensive. We made ends meet with temporary jobs, but not for long. Our friend "Frieder" called to ask me if I was interested in a secretarial job with the Institute for Mathematical Sciences at New York University. What a question! I immediately took the job, and for the next twenty years I was involved in very interesting work at the institute.

"Frieder" was not our friend's real name. His wife, Nellie, did not like his actual name, Kurt Otto Friedrichs, and changed his first name to Frieder. Everybody liked the name; even his colleagues called him that. Nellie was one of my original "fans" in Braunschweig (she is much younger than I) and became my friend. In Braunschweig I had known her mother and grandmother, two very well-educated, refined women. I had been very much impressed with their child-rearing methods. For example, when Nellie received a present, her friend, a child of less well-to-do parents, was immediately given the same. This upbringing had a great influence on Nellie's way of dealing with people in later life. She was always considerate and ready to lend a helping hand. She visited me in Vienna and later again in Darmstadt. After graduating high school, she studied child psychology at the Technical University of Braunschweig. During the annual New Year's Ball, a young man, whom she took for a student, asked her to dance. As she found out subsequently, he was a math professor—and that was Frieder. They became very close. Unfortunately, it was just at the beginning of the Nazis' rise to power. Nellie was Jewish, though Frieder wasn't. They both knew that their relationship could be dangerous, and they met secretly in other towns, sometimes at the home of courageous friends. Finally, they decided to emigrate to America, where they planned to get married. Frieder's former teacher and friend, Richard Courant, a well-known mathematician, had promised him a position. At first, Frieder applied for extended leave, but with the intention never to return; it was denied. Then they found another solution. Since Nellie's father was a Frenchman who lived in Lyon, she was able to live in that country without difficulties. From France she went to New York. Frieder waited for his vacation, then he packed a small suitcase and took the same route. His sister was on vacation in France, so he easily obtained an exit visa. From there he took a ship to America, where Nellie was waiting for him. They both obtained visas for Canada, and on the way back, they found a justice of the peace in a small town who married them.

Meanwhile, Professor Courant became director of the Graduate Department at New York University. He warned the American government about the threat of another world war and convinced the authorities of the urgent need to modernize the department. Shortly after the outbreak of the war, the government took his advice, and a few years later the Courant Institute for Mathematical Sciences was established. Our friend Frieder had a teaching and research position there as well.

How prominent our friend was in his field became clear to us during a summer stay in Chicago. Wolfgang had a three-month appointment at some school to teach acting. It may have been around 1940. We needed an apartment, and I looked through the posted ads at the university. We were lucky to find somebody who wanted to sublet for the summer. The area was very good, close to the Midway, Chicago's broad, gardenlike commons. Within half an hour, the apartment was ours for the next three months, but with an important proviso: our new landlord asked, somewhat embarrassed, if his wife could stay in the apartment. She was five months pregnant, and shied away from the trip and a new environment. Since they both seemed very pleasant, we agreed and never had a reason to regret it.

When the business had been taken care off, we spoke about this and that, and thus we learned that the expectant father was a mathematician. When we told him about our friend who also was a mathematician, he wanted to know his name. We assured him that he could not possibly know him since he had been in America only two years. "If he has published, I'll know his name," Will insisted. When I said "Friedrichs," he jumped up as if electrified and asked, "K. O. Friedrichs?" And when we answered in the affirmative, we were showered with a lecture: "In that case, I must enlighten you. He is not only a mathematician. He is something very special. *Every* mathematician knows his name. Just imagine a pyramid with a peak formed by three, maybe four." He mentioned three names: Siegel, von Neumann, Wiener—all of which became household names for me later. "If he is not number four, which is possible, then he is on the next platform of ten. Then follow fifty, a thousand, and in the end ten thousand. And one of those is me." He must have been right, for over the years, Frieder was awarded five honorary doctorates in various countries. He also was the recipient of the National Medal of Science, the American substitute for the missing Nobel Prize in mathematics. Under President Carter, Frieder was honored with the National Medal of Honor that had been instituted by President Kennedy.

It was typical of our friend that we were left in the dark about his prominence before this chance discovery in Chicago. He was one of the most modest men I have ever known. Besides repeated visits in the course of the year, we always spent Christmas together. I don't think that we would even have celebrated Christmas had it not been for this wonderful family and their wish to have our company. Nellie's mother had her own small apartment in the house, and then there were gradually five endearing children—our substitute children. Each child made something by hand—later they bought something—for everybody, and the adults made or bought something for all five. It was overwhelmingly touching to see the children open their presents and to open our presents from them. Later we had the privilege to witness each child develop into a remarkable individual. Nellie was an extraordinary mother and pedagogue, and she proves this again now with regard to her grandchildren. Frieder participated fully in raising the children. Every day he spent an extra hour with the children in his room, either in front of the blackboard or in animated discussion. All five showed their love and appreciation in a very moving eulogy during a memorial service after his death in 1982.

I have always maintained that I have a hole in the head where others have a place for math. Thus it should hardly be surprising that I started my new job with a great deal of trepidation, although Frieder had assured me that I would have nothing to do with mathematics. I had to make appointments for students who wanted to see him, write his letters, sell the famous "notes," the student aids written by members of the institute. I was perfectly up to tasks of this sort and actually liked doing them. This whole new world was an eye-opener for me. The relationship between students and professors as I knew it from Germany was a rather stiff one compared to the casual tone that existed here. I found the whole atmosphere very pleasant. The young assistants, who almost all became renowned scientists, treated me as one of their own—and still do. All were on a first-name basis. Maybe a similar atmosphere exists in Germany today. If so, then it is probably due to the American influence. For me, back then, all this was a very pleasant surprise.

Professor Courant knew of my acting past, and when I was unexpectedly called for an audition one day, he urged me to take the job if it were offered to me. Arrangements could easily be made. And thus it happened that for one year I played a Swedish housekeeper in a soap opera. Since the rehearsals took place early in the morning on workdays—about twice a week—I would be half an hour late for work at most and would take a shorter lunch hour. Such a relaxed arrangement was quite typical of the atmosphere at the institute. I am certain I could not have found a better place to work.

At the end of twenty years I bade my farewell. I had felt quite at home at the institute, but in time I began to tire more easily and felt the need to sleep longer in the morning or to read or take walks in the park. But nothing much came of that. I am unable to explain why, but to this very day I find very little time to read or to walk in the park. It is true I have a few new responsibilities: four "lame ducks"—as Galsworthy calls them—four old ladies in their nineties whom I visit regularly, unless I am busy with an occasional job in my chosen profession. For example, I played a dying woman in *All That Jazz* (1979), a sick old woman in *Tattoo* (1981), and the like. Once, almost by accident, I got a small part in the film *Marathon Man* (1976). It so happened that, one day, a casting director whom I knew called and asked for Wolfgang, who wasn't home then. I wrote down all the details and asked in passing whether there was also a part for an old woman with a German accent. The obliging agent said yes, there was one indeed. He would arrange a meeting with the director, John Schlesinger. I waited in suspense. The prospect of getting a role with this director was incredibly exciting, for I appreciated his work very much. At long last the agent called about an audition. When I entered the waiting room, another woman with beautiful black eyes was already there. She was dressed all in black and wore a black hat. My heart sank. This was exactly how I had imagined the character from the agent's description.

I was handed a few pages of text. It was a small but good role. A weary old woman hurries down 47th Street and screams incessantly, "Der weiße Engel, Dr. Szell, der weiße Engel!" ("The white angel, Dr. Szell, the white angel!") As she does this, she points at a man, played by Laurence Olivier, who had tortured her and others in a concentration camp. (The character was based on the then-still-living Dr. Mengele, who was called the "angel of death" of Auschwitz.)

Strangely enough, I was called first. John Schlesinger asked me to read the lines, or, if I preferred, I should just improvise. I did both. When I was done, he said, "Wonderful." Naturally I was very pleased to hear him say that. But I thought of the waiting woman and said, "I am glad to hear you say this, but I am sure you will give the part to the other woman in the waiting room. She looks absolutely wonderful." Whereupon he burst into laughter and asked, "Does that mean you wouldn't accept the role if I offered it to you?" To which I replied quickly, "I wouldn't go that far." And we left it at that for the time being.

I heard nothing, and after a while I told myself that the "woman in black" must have gotten the part. But about five weeks later I received a call from the costume department, asking me to come for a fitting. I asked, perplexed, "How so? Does this mean I got the part?" The person at the other end of the line responded, equally perplexed, "Well, on my list it says: 'Old Woman on 47th Street.' Isn't that you?" And I, extremely happy, replied, "Exactly. That's me." And thus my name was on the casting list.

One day when I had to show Schlesinger my costume, he said with a broad grin: "Well, are you angry with me for picking you over the other woman?" "Of course not," I replied. "But she looked wonderful." Then he added with a serious tone: "She looked wonderful, but you *were* wonderful."

Unfortunately, Wolfgang did not get the role for which he had been called. But my role was very important to me for several reasons. For one, it was a great pleasure to be able to work with John Schlesinger. And second, after the film came out, people recognized me in the street and would sometimes greet me with something like "Da wassa Enkel" and would shake my hand—something like that feels good in an actor's heart. The best part of it was that I met Laurence Olivier. I knew that he was playing the monstrous Dr. Szell, but I did not expect to have the opportunity to speak with him since he had to walk along the opposite side of the street, and after each take everybody tended to disappear into the dressing rooms. But fate arranged it differently. Mr. Olivier had for some time been very ill. The Gotham Bookstore on 47th Street—I believe it is the oldest and best bookstore in New York—offered to have him stay between takes in a comfortable room in the back of the store. To my surprise, I, too, was invited. I seated myself far away from the star, and did not look at him, since I did not want to impose. But he did not leave it at that. Suddenly I heard his voice. I looked up and realized that he called me over to him. Obediently, I followed the invitation. We had an animated discussion. Others followed, and there was even a kiss when we said good-bye. And now I am even the happy owner of two letters.

The last, but by no means least, surprise came from one of those strange coincidences in life that make it all so interesting. Two ladies were sitting with me in the trailer that served as the dressing room.

While they were talking, I suddenly heard one of them ask the actress Estelle Omens for the name of her husband. When I heard the answer, "Frank Gregory," I jumped up and called out, "I know him!" Estelle replied soberly, "There are at least a dozen Frank Gregorys." I replied with more composure, "Well, mine went to Italy; he was the director of *Girls in Uniform*." "That's mine!" exclaimed Estelle. Now it was her turn to jump up. "What is your name? I'll call him right away." I gave her my name and added, "Tell him that I am today that which I played then: an old woman." Soon thereafter we met. By an even greater coincidence, we lived only two streets away from each other. This is typical of New York: one has neighbors, but one never runs into them. We became good friends, the four of us: Frank and Wolfgang, Estelle and Lotte, until they moved to California because Estelle thought the opportunities for her career were better there. Whenever I visited my sister, about twice a year, we would get together. Then one day Frank told me that his wife was very ill, and a short time later she died. That Estelle, with her joie de vivre, so alive and happy with Frank, always in a cheerful mood, should be dead! It was incomprehensible. Frank visited us alone or with friends. One day "a little kitten" joined the circle—a charming, witty, original artist. Today they are Mr. and Mrs. Gregory, and I love them both.

After *Marathon Man* there was a long period with nothing. My frustration grew despite the fact that I was aware that at my age and with my accent I could not expect much for the future. One day I decided to do something about it. Ever since Wolfgang and I had begun receiving restitution payments from Germany, we put something away whenever possible, and with time we had saved a tidy sum. I decided to invest my share in a small film project with myself in the main role. The first order of business was to find a story. I thought I had found the right one when I read *Das Wunschkonzert* (*The Command Performance*) by Franz Xaver Kroetz. It was a silent, one-act play, accompanied only by the music of the "command performance." It seemed quite suited to me. Next I had to find a crew. I spoke to my young friend Peter Almond, who had been assistant producer for movies at Channel 13. He liked the piece and thought it wouldn't cost too much since the plot centered on only one person. He also knew other young people who would be only too happy to collaborate in a cooperative venture. As director we selected an Israeli with whom Wolfgang had worked on a student film production. He enthusiastically endorsed the idea.

The next step was to obtain the rights. I explained the project to the author, Mr. Kroetz, in a letter, introduced my coworkers, told him about myself (six-year acting career in Germany, Jewish, emigrant, and so on) as well as about the cooperative. No reply. I wrote a second letter. When this one, too, remained unanswered, I asked a friend in Munich to get Mr. Kroetz's telephone number for me. After the third letter, Peter lost his patience. He called and left a message on the answering machine that he would call again at such and such a time. This call, too, was without result. I was about to give up the whole thing, even though this one-act play seemed made for me: a silent movie, thus no accent difficulties, but a moving drama. So I decided on a last-ditch attack: I asked my friend in Munich to try to get in touch with Kroetz directly. And, surprisingly, he got what had been denied us. Mr. Kroetz answered the door himself and promised to write us a letter. After another long period of apprehensive waiting, the reply came: he gave us permission on the condition that we pay him $40,000 before we start shooting the film. I must admit, I never answered the letter.

Peter, his friend Steve Brier, our coproducer, and I met in Peter's office. It was a depressing conference. In the end I got up and said jokingly, "Well, then, you just have to write something for Wolfgang and me." Peter and his assistant, Nancy Musser, immediately put together a script, which we liked very much: *A Private Life.* Since our director had meanwhile returned to Israel, I suggested that Peter hire the Russian Mikhail Bogin. We had greatly admired his film *Ballad of Love* and were very happy when he agreed, after he had seen the completed script. The filming started in March 1979, six months after I had first spoken to Peter.

The crew of sixteen people—most of them very young—formed a very harmonious group. Some worked for nothing but still applied themselves with the same enthusiasm as those few who did receive a small honorarium. We had a wonderful time, and I must say that I would have been happy with the work even if nothing more had ever come of it. But the creation of the film was like an obstacle course. There were technical difficulties, illnesses, accidents, and after a few weeks we ran out of money. Several people had to leave for other projects since production ceased for a quite a while. Fortunately, we had enough material to show to the Council of the Arts. We received a grant, and the project was finally completed. Apparently we had done something right, because the film received three first prizes, and the Museum of Modern Art bought it for its archives. For Wolfgang and me there was no gain. But several of our coworkers, all Americans, did gain some benefit—and thus everything was well.

It was the best of times—it was the worst of times—it was the year 1987. I had been invited the year before by the Jewish Community of Berlin to read an abbreviated version of my memoirs. (The larger part had not been written down yet.) To my great surprise, Gero Gandert, who was mentioned in it, showed the manuscript to somebody in Berlin and an invitation followed.

Since a trip from New York to Berlin was not an everyday affair, I decided to visit my family in their Swiss vacation place. From there we went to their house in Ville d'Avray, a suburb of Paris. Then I went to Düsseldorf to see my friend Lore Ketzler. She was, I must say, a "legacy" of my friend Wanda Kampmann from my school days in Essen. We were both commuters—she came from Wattenscheid and I from Bochum. We met sometimes on the early morning train and became friends. After the war I heard that she had gone through rough times because she did not want to take part in the Hitler craze. She had to leave her teaching post and fled with her aging mother to a Bavarian village. I was deeply touched by this story. I renewed our contact, which we had already lost before 1933 due to the great divergence in the careers we pursued. As it turned out, the years had not separated us; if anything, they had brought us closer together. And whenever I was in Europe to visit my family, I also met with Wanda, if only to spend some time with her or to travel with her to a nearby place. This is how I met my younger friend Lore, with whom I maintained a close friendship after Wanda's all-too-untimely death. Through these two women I got to know more people who had the same attitude, and now I know that there were—and still are—other Germans as well, not only those who murdered my mother. After seeing Lore, I planned to get together with two of my "Braunschweig girls," and then travel on to Berlin.

I love to travel in Europe by rail. The trains are clean, comfortable, and on time—one can set one's watch by them. Before I boarded the train, I checked my big suitcase. I had packed a lot of clothes, warm for Zermatt, light for Germany, and many presents for my friends in Berlin, among them numerous books, which added to its weight. To my horror, I learned in Düsseldorf that the suitcase had been stolen. It was never recovered. In its place I received, after a year, a small sum with which I was able to replace some of the lost items. But many personal mementos were lost.

Yet this was not the greatest catastrophe that hit me. That one reached me on the second day after my arrival. Lore met me at the station in the company of a young friend I did not know. I thought Lore quite changed. She leaned heavily on her friend, who drove us home in her car and then left immediately so we could be alone. We did not chat very long because I was very tired. But the next day, Lore's behavior appeared strange to me. At times she made outright hostile remarks, only to erase them immediately with kindness. I knew my friend had already suffered twice from manic-depressive episodes, and it occurred to me that maybe she was having a recurrence. I called Inge's sister Marlis, also one of Lore's friends in Düsseldorf. She came right away. It was evening meanwhile. She, too, thought that Lore was ill and called her psychotherapist, who asked Lore to come to the telephone to persuade her to come to the clinic. What surprised me, and at the same time gave me the feeling that this was the best solution, was Lore's readiness to follow the advice of her doctor. She had asked her diplomatically, "Do you think it would be best for you to come to the clinic? Do you remember how good you had it there a few years ago?" Lore nodded and followed like a lamb. Marlis and I took her to the clinic together, stayed with her another hour, and then left with heavy hearts.

Marlis took me home, that is, back to Lore's empty apartment, and stayed with me for a while. I understood that she couldn't stay longer since she had to cook for her husband and two boys. Besides, friends had planned a birthday party for her. Would I come? I had an appointment elsewhere and asked Marlis to excuse me. I was completely at my wit's end. I wanted nothing more than to depart right away. But Marlis did not give up. She called early in the afternoon and urged me to come. Both times I thanked her, but I just did not feel up to meeting so many strangers. About six o'clock the telephone rang again: "Please, Lotte, do come. I don't like to see you all by yourself." I said, "You are very kind. But I am just not up to it. I am just washing my dress." Whereupon I heard a burst of laughter at the other end of the line, and I couldn't help but chime in. It really was a funny situation. I was washing the dress I was wearing not out of a compulsion for laundering but for practical reasons. I had nothing to change into—my suitcase had been stolen—and after three hot days, my dress simply needed washing. Following Marlis's advice, I took a dress from Lore's wardrobe, which was much too big for me, and pinned it together somehow. I was just in time for the birthday feast, and, most important, I met a group of people there whom I would not like to have missed. I shall never forget this evening. I believe that without the kindness of Lore's friend, I, too, would have had a nervous breakdown.

Before her retirement Lore had been director of a law school, and it was the professors and their wives, besides Inge and another woman, with whom I spent the evening. They received me like an old friend, and I felt very much at home in the company of these intelligent, interesting people. I admired their loyalty. Marlis's husband, a historian, managed the visitors' list for Lore so that she would have some daily diversion at the clinic. A mathematician managed the financial affairs, such as paying bills or cashing incoming checks. Each one made some contribution so that Lore had nothing to be concerned about for the length of her stay at the clinic, which was almost a year.

I remained in Düsseldorf for a week. My "suitcase tragedy" was trivial next to Lore's breakdown. Every day Inge, that good soul, drove me to the train station, where I inquired about my suitcase, but without success. She also took me to the city a few times to shop for clothes, but with equal lack of success. There was nothing either of us liked, and so I decided to wait until I got to Berlin. But that, too, took a different turn. Inge invited me to dinner at her pretty apartment and offered me a beautiful gray, two-piece dress that was too tight on her and that she had wanted to give to a friend in East Germany. I accepted under the condition that she would give my suit to her friend. (Better a used but still good piece of clothing than a much-worn one.)

Then I received a call from Marianne Hermann, a woman I had met at the birthday party, who offered to have me borrow anything from her wardrobe I wished. Thus, with the help of these benefactors, I reached Berlin with fewer but more elegant clothes than I could have found in my suitcase.

All my life I have had the best of luck with human beings, but never have I experienced such a warmhearted mass reception. When I finally had time to think about it, I found a rather logical explanation. Most of these people, maybe even all of them, were in the Hitler Youth when they were young. They presumably experienced grave doubts later and became aware of Hitler's heinous crimes. It is, therefore, quite possible that their behavior toward me was something of an act of "restitution." But this does by no means diminish their merit; on the contrary, it increases it. I hope they shall always remain my friends.

When it was finally confirmed that my suitcase was irretrievably lost, I made my way to Braunschweig to see my "girls" there. We spent a wonderful time together in the beautiful old hotel, where in my day the annual theater balls were held. Then I took the train to Berlin. There, everything went very smoothly. During the first week I stayed with my friends Erika and Ulrich Gregor. Unfortunately, they had to leave after two days to attend one of many film festivals—I had misunderstood the dates of their schedule—in order to track down foreign and partly experimental films for the Arsenal Theater, which they managed for the German Cinémathèque. After a week, which I spent with their daughter Milena and old Berlin friends, I moved into the Kempinski. Then followed a week filled to bursting with activities: I saw movies, visited exhibits, attended the theater, went to lectures and concerts, and all that as a guest of the Jewish Community! When the day of my reading arrived, Gero Gandert said to me, probably to spare me any disappointment, "Don't be surprised if attendance is low. Tonight everybody in this town is likely to be sitting in front of the 'tube' to hear what Mr. Honecker has to say to Mr. Kohl." He was right. Only about thirty or forty people were present. They seemed to like my life's story as well as our short film, since I was invited to give radio and television interviews on several stations. In December I was visited by four nice young people who made a longish documentary shoot for the program *Mosaik*.

One more surprise was in store for me during this fateful year. The beginning of this story goes back a few years. Wolfgang had for some time been developing Parkinson's disease, and, as is well known, this terrible disease not only changes the body but frequently also the character of the afflicted person. I had the feeling that Wolfgang asked himself, "Why me—and not her?" However this may be, our relationship had changed over the years, and one day, in 1984, he declared that he wanted to live in a nursing home in Germany—but alone. I was speechless at first, but then I said quietly, "I would, of course, have accompanied you—reluctantly, after all that has happened there—but now I am relieved that you want to go alone."

We asked around for a good home and found one on the recommendation of our friend Dietrichs in Berlin. We looked at each other, and on August 1, 1985, we took the plane to Berlin, I for a week, Wolfgang for two years. The Heinrich-Gruber House turned out to be very good. In 1986 Wolfgang came back to New York for a visit, accompanied by a nurse, Sister Monika, because he was no longer able to travel by himself. We spent several comfortable weeks together. Monika loved New York. I was glad that Wolfgang had found a good nurse, for I was no longer able to perform many of the small tasks that were necessary. I noticed too that their relationship went beyond the nursing level. A few weeks later they departed.

We stayed in contact, and when I was in Berlin in 1987, Wolfgang declared that he wanted to marry Monika, move out of the home, and go back to New York with her. But, so he said, he couldn't expect her to give up her job. She also told me that she loved him too much to let him go all by himself. I had no real objections as long as Wolfgang was taken care of, since we had once again become the best of friends. And as it happened, they returned to New York in October of the same year. I filed for divorce, which became final in spring of 1988. And so ended that eventful year.

The highlight of the following year was an invitation from my nephew and his wife to spend two weeks with them in the Canadian Rockies. Two years before, we had been on vacation together, their three children included, in the western parks of the United States, and all had been harmonious and wonderful. This time the children were at camp to learn English—thanks to Hitler, they are all French!—but their parents speak English as well.

I was happy that I was invited. Since they are mountain climbers and were taking longer hikes than I was able to keep up with, we started out together and I accompanied them as far as I could. Then I stayed back. I had a quiet, leisurely lunch, which my niece Arlette packed for me, or I would go to a snack bar where I met all sorts of people—Americans, French, Canadians, and others—and I would have a chat for an hour or so. Sometimes I sat in the woods and read or just enjoyed the beautiful countryside. My life's myriad events passed before me—the good and the bad, as everyone experienced it. And one day, I took a pen from my pocket and began to write on a brown paper bag.

The largest part of my memoirs, the Hitler time, I had read in Berlin. One of those present, the writer and journalist Stefan Lorant, said to me afterward, "You must continue to write; you have a story to tell." He lives in Lenox, Massachusetts, and he called me now and then: "Are you writing?" My answer was always no. So we quarreled for almost two years—and now I am sitting in Canada, writing. And it actually gives me pleasure!

I remember how Victor had often tried to console me in the most difficult times: "One day we will laugh about many of the absurd things that are happening to us." I was glad that I had actually arrived at that point. I thought of America, where we had found a refuge and work—even if it was not exactly the way we had hoped. I thought of my friends in New York. Because of them, this city had become my chosen hometown—not my true home. I thought of my friends everywhere, in England, in France, in Spain, emigrants like me. I thought of Wanda, who did not want to play the game anymore . . .

And Germany, my erstwhile home? I thought of the dear Gregors in Berlin, my new friends in Düsseldorf; I thought of the Gunßers who took me in with such warmth. I know now that there were and still are other Germans than those who murdered my mother and drove out or martyred millions of our fellow Jews. And yet, I am not at home in Germany anymore. How could I be after all those horrifying events? Am I then homeless? I don't believe so. My home is where my friends are. My hymn goes:

Friendship, friendship above everything,
Above everything in the world!

✻

Jewish Lives